Multi-Play

Sensory Activities
for School Readiness

by
Gerri A. Duran, OTR/L, and
Sharon Klenke-Ormiston, M.A., CCC-SLP

Illustrations completed under contract by Corwyn Zimbleman

Therapy Skill Builders
A division of
Communication Skill Builders
3830 E. Bellevue/P.O. Box 42050
Tucson, Arizona 85733/(602) 323-7500

Reproducing Pages from This Book

The Possible Trouble Signs list can be reproduced for instructional or administrative use (not for resale). To protect your book, make a photocopy of this reproducible page. Then use that copy as a master for photocopying or other types of reproduction.

© 1994 by

Therapy Skill Builders
A division of
Communication Skill Builders
3830 E. Bellevue/P.O. Box 42050
Tucson, Arizona 85733/(602) 323-7500

ISBN 0-88450-657-6   Catalog No. 4306

10 9 8 7 6 5 4 3 2 1
Printed in the United States of America

For information about our audio and/or video products, write us at:
Therapy Skill Builders, P.O. Box 42050, Tucson, AZ 85733.

Special Thanks

- To the administration and staff of Mountainair Public Schools, New Mexico, and to the staff of Cooperative Educational Services (especially to Max, David, and Chris). Much appreciation is also given to our families and to Tom for their continued support and understanding.

- To fellow professionals (especially Sharon Schnupp, Rich Shine, and Nancy Brinkley), who provided invaluable input and encouragement.

About the Authors

Gerri A. Duran is a native of Albuquerque, New Mexico, where she practices occupational therapy. A graduate of the University of Kansas, she works in a variety of settings which include the newborn intensive care nursery, adolescent and adult psychiatric facilities, and rural New Mexico schools. While working in the public schools, she observed the overlap between the caseloads of occupational therapy and speech therapy. Her experiences providing team therapy with a speech-language pathologist have convinced her of the benefits of transdisciplinary therapy.

Sharon Klenke-Ormiston is a speech-language pathologist currently practicing in New Mexico. She was born in Fort Wayne, Indiana, and attended Purdue University at both the Fort Wayne and the West Lafayette campuses, where she received her bachelor's degree in communication disorders. She received her master's degree in speech-language pathology from Ball State University in Muncie, Indiana. It was while working at the Fort Wayne State Hospital and Training Center during the 1960s and 1970s that she realized the value of movement in enhancing the development of speech and language skills. Since moving to New Mexico, she has worked with hearing impaired individuals in a private clinic, provided services in rural public schools, and developed a private practice.

Contents

Introduction

Multi-Play provides activities that supplement a kindergarten curriculum and enhance specific speech, language, and motor skills. These activities are designed for classroom use and are appropriate for normally developing children as well as children with a variety of mild to moderate language and learning difficulties. They may be used by regular classroom teachers, special education teachers, speech-language pathologists, occupational therapists, physical therapists, or any combination of these professionals.

Extensive research substantiates that sensation and movement facilitate language and learning, particularly in an academic setting. Infants learn through movement and from the consequences of their movements. Because of this, motor development has far-reaching implications for learning. For the entering kindergartner, the combination of sensorimotor and language tasks duplicates the child's familiar and natural means of acquiring skills. Typical kindergartners learn most effectively when they use all of their senses concomitantly—vision, hearing, touch, movement, and others. Therefore, the activities in this book stimulate a variety of senses in order to improve language, motor, and academic functioning. These activities also incorporate a number of different concepts that are typical of a child's natural play experiences.

Collaborative teaching is a philosophy that is becoming familiar to more professionals every day. Many schools are requesting that speech-language pathologists enter the classroom and team teach with the teacher. The resulting exchange of information between the two disciplines has had a positive effect on students' learning. Collaboration between speech-language pathologists and occupational therapists in traditional "pull-out" therapy settings has also proven effective.

Multi-Play combines these collaborative approaches. Consider the amount that children learn between birth and five years of age through movement and the consequences of their movement. Having children sit in their chairs for six hours each day, passively listening rather than actively learning, is not an effective means of teaching. These activities offer an alternative to passive learning; they combine movement with language skills to support learning in the areas of reading readiness, math readiness, and language and listening.

A field study was conducted to compare the skills of two similar kindergarten classes in the areas of speech-language and motor improvement. Both classes were taught by the same teacher. The control class received the standard school curriculum. In addition to the standard curriculum, the treatment group received supplementary activities that reinforce curriculum concepts. Many of the activities in this book were used with the students in the experimental group.

Pre- and post-testing was completed with both classes to measure the following speech-language and motor skills: balance, motor planning, articulation in words and in sentences, auditory memory, and auditory discrimination. The pre- and post-tests consisted of items selected from various standardized motor and speech-language assessments. No significant differences were found in the pre-test scores for the control and the treatment groups. On post-testing, the treatment group showed greater improvement in all five areas assessed. Analysis of covariance indicated that the treatment group's scores were significantly higher than those of the control group for auditory discrimination of words and praxis as well as total score.

These results suggest that incorporating language-motor activities in the regular classroom curriculum facilitates development of skills which are necessary for effective learning.

Overview of the Book

The purpose of *Multi-Play* is to provide you with enjoyable activities that will complement the classroom curriculum without requiring significant planning time. The activities in the book are arranged in alphabetical order by title. Immediately beneath the title is indicated the skill area or areas targeted in that activity: reading readiness, language and listening, or math readiness. More specific skills addressed within the activity are also listed, including academic, sensorimotor, and speech-language skills necessary for effective learning.

Materials

The materials needed for each activity are listed as well as an estimation of the time required to complete the activity. Naturally, the time will vary depending upon the size of your class and how you conduct the activity.

Levels

Because of the variability in development among individual children and the differences between the skills of an entering kindergartner and an exiting kindergartner, directions are given for presenting each activity in this book at entry, intermediate, and advanced levels. Use your clinical judgment in determining which version of each activity to use with your class. Depending upon your students' skills, the particular activity, and the concept being reinforced, you may decide to use one level or a combination of levels—you know your students and how they respond best.

Be flexible and creative in the use of these activities, taking into account the personalities and abilities of the children in your class. Several of the activities can be modified to address areas other than those we have suggested; feel free to "mix and match" components of the activities and objectives. An example of such an adaptation appears in the activities "Alpha-Ball" and "Number Ball" (see pages 21 and 69). The same basic activity is used to address the areas of reading readiness and math readiness, respectively.

"Jiffies" are activities that can be conducted within a time frame of roughly five minutes. Although these activities are short, they address the same fundamental concepts stressed in the longer activities. Jiffies are useful when your children are waiting in line—something they do many times throughout the day—or whenever you have a few minutes to kill.

Following the Jiffies section are Excitatory and Calming activities. These activities do not address specific curriculum goals. Rather, as their names imply, these activities will tend either to increase or reduce children's energy levels. These activities are particularly useful for transitions where children have to significantly change their activity levels—for example, when they return to the classroom after recess.

Selecting Activities

Immediately following the introduction are five tables, one for each of the academic areas of reading readiness, language and listening, and math readiness, plus specific motor and speech-language goals. Each table lists, in alphabetical order, all the activities that pertain to the particular academic or therapy area. The "✔"s indicate specific goal areas that the activity addresses. *All* the activities involve listening, following directions, and social skills. Therefore, only the activities that focus directly on following specific directions are listed under "Following Directions" in the Language and Listening table. You will find that several activities appear in more than one table, because they are relevant to more than one skill area.

A Note to the Motor Therapist

With the advent of inclusion, occupational and physical therapists are increasingly being expected to provide services for students on their caseloads together with children who are not on their caseloads. The Guide to Motor and Sensorimotor

Activities allows occupational and physical therapists to identify activities that address specific treatment areas of individual children while improving the motor skills of the entire class. The goal areas listed in this guide are ones that therapists frequently include in the IEPs of children on their caseloads. It is important to remember that these activities simultaneously incorporate curricular and speech-language components that may be difficult for some children. In this case, it may be necessary to adapt the activities.

A Note to the Speech-Language Pathologist

Working with a large group of children presents a challenge for most speech-language pathologists. We hope that the activities in this book will make the collaborative approach not only easy but fun.

Every activity in this book requires communication with the students, so they can all be used to address the basic skills of listening, socializing, and following directions. In addition, many of the academic areas listed under Reading Readiness and Math Readiness also overlap with language development. For example, under Reading Readiness, you will find color recognition, directionality/prepositions, and same/different. All the goals listed in the curriculum area of Language and Listening are related to skills that speech-language pathologists regularly target in therapy sessions.

In addition to the "academic areas," many activities incorporate other, more specific language-development goals. These goals are listed in the Guide to Speech and Language Activities. Speech-language pathologists can pick and choose from all these guides to target a variety of language skills in the regular kindergarten classroom. We encourage you to use these activities creatively and to adapt them in whatever ways will make them most effective in your situation.

Possible Trouble Signs

Because kindergarten teachers are in contact with children at the beginning of their academic careers, they are in an ideal position to intercede on behalf of children who may require special intervention. Therefore we have provided the following lists of speech-language and sensorimotor behaviors that indicate a possible problem area in development. We strongly recommend that teachers consult with the appropriate ancillary personnel regarding students who consistently show any of these behaviors more frequently than their peers. If you are not a classroom teacher yourself, you may photocopy these lists to give to the teachers with whom you work.

Possible Trouble Signs

The behaviors listed here may indicate a delay in speech-language or sensorimotor skills. If you notice students who show these behaviors more often than the other children in your class, we suggest you consult with the speech-language pathologist or occupational therapist as appropriate.

Speech-Language Behaviors

1. *Listening*
   - Often needs to have directions and questions repeated
   - Often does not seem to understand directions and questions (for example, frequently asks "what?")
   - Repeats or echoes what others say
   - Has difficulty attending to what is being said
   - Has difficulty answering questions (for example, may give the wrong type of information in response)
   - Takes an unusually long time to respond

2. *Speaking*
   - Is difficult to understand
   - Uses incorrect pronouns (for example, "Me want . . .")
   - Has trouble repeating sentences
   - Leaves words out of sentences (for example, "That not right.")
   - Has difficulty naming or describing things

3. *Reasoning*
   - Has difficulty formulating thoughts (overuses "uh" and "um")
   - Has trouble understanding concepts
   - Has many false starts in sentences

continued

Possible Trouble Signs (continued)

Sensorimotor Behaviors

- Recoils from touch, especially that which is light or unexpected
- Falls out of or off chairs or equipment
- Trips, falls, or runs into objects
- Is unusually fearful of heights or movement (does not like feet to leave the ground)
- Seems to crave excessive movement or places self in precarious situations
- Slumps over work rather than sitting upright when doing seat work
- Shows extreme disorganization in work spaces
- Cannot grasp concept of working from left to right (for example, always begins in the middle or on the right side of the paper)
- Has difficulty using both hands together in tasks that require two hands
- Frequently gets lost when going from one room to another
- Shows considerably poorer quality of movement on one side of the body than the other side

Guide to Reading Readiness Activities

	Page	Color Recognition	Directionality/Prepositions	Letter Recognition	Patterns/Sequencing	Phonics	Rhyming	Same/Different	Shape Recognition	Word/Name Recognition
Alpha-Ball	21			✔		✔				
Back Scrambles	24		✔	✔	✔				✔	
Balloon Matching	28	✔		✔	✔				✔	
Bean Socks	30	✔								
Clappy Days	32									✔
Connect the Children	34								✔	
Cotton Ball Blews	36	✔								
Do You Hear What I Hear?	38				✔					
Echo Clap J	105				✔					
Flamingo Fandango J	106		✔							
Harvesting Descriptors	41	✔								
Hop-Along Letters	43			✔		✔				
Hopping to Feel	44							✔		
Hoppity Different	46			✔				✔		
Hop to It J	107	✔		✔						
Human Bowling Pins	48			✔	✔				✔	
Identify Yourself	50			✔						✔
Macrame Writing	57		✔	✔						✔
Measure and Compare	58							✔		
Memory Coursing	60			✔						
Musical Ball	62	✔		✔	✔					
Name and Describe	66	✔								✔
Plates of Shapes	74	✔						✔	✔	

J = Jiffies

continued

Guide to Reading Readiness Activities
(continued)

	Page	Color Recognition	Directionality/Prepositions	Letter Recognition	Patterns/Sequencing	Phonics	Rhyming	Same/Different	Shape Recognition	Word/Name Recognition
Plates of Shapes Revisited	77	✔							✔	
Prep-O-Ball	80		✔	✔						
Prepositional Freeze	81		✔							
Prepositions with Rhythm	82		✔					✔		
Rhyme Time	83						✔			
Rhyming Hops ᴶ	109						✔			
Same Noise/Different Noise ᴶ	109							✔		
Scooterboard Flash	84			✔						
Shopping Spree	86	✔		✔	✔				✔	
Strung Along	88		✔							
Targeting Sounds	91			✔		✔				
Vocal Play ᴶ	111					✔				
Walking the Plank	96		✔							
Wheelbarrow Memory	97				✔					
Word Hopping	100			✔		✔	✔			

ᴶ = Jiffies

Guide to Language and Listening Activities

	Page	Body Part Identification	Descriptor Use	Following Directions	Inferences	Listening	Object Classification	Prediction	Sentence Usage	Time Concepts
Absurd Tug-o-War	19					✔			✔	
Animal House	23			✔			✔		✔	
Appliance Alive[J]	104		✔							
Balloon Body Parts	26	✔		✔						
Bean Socks	30	✔	✔				✔			
Clappy Days	32	✔								✔
Connect the Children	34						✔			
Do You Hear What I Hear?	38					✔				
Echo Clap[J]	105					✔				
Fishing for an Occupation	39	✔			✔				✔	
Harvesting Descriptors	41	✔					✔			
Hopping to Feel	44	✔				✔	✔		✔	
Hoppity Different	46	✔							✔	
Hop to It[J]	107	✔							✔	
I Am Going . . .[J]	108						✔		✔	
If the Lid Fits . . .	51	✔			✔			✔	✔	
Jet Set Shopping	53						✔			
Judge for Yourself	54	✔				✔	✔			
Key Word Stories	56	✔			✔				✔	
Measure and Compare	58	✔						✔		
Memory Coursing	60			✔	✔				✔	✔
Musical Ball	62					✔				
Musical Chair Descriptions	64	✔			✔	✔			✔	

[J] = Jiffies

continued

Guide to Language and Listening Activities

(continued)

	Page	Body Part Identification	Descriptor Use	Following Directions	Inferences	Listening	Object Classification	Prediction	Sentence Usage	Time Concepts
Name and Describe	66		✔						✔	
Name That Time	67								✔	✔
Penny for Your Thoughts	70	✔						✔		
Pinning with a Song	72	✔	✔		✔					
Plates of Shapes	74		✔	✔						
Plates of Shapes Revisited	77							✔	✔	
Prep-O-Ball	80		✔							
Prepositional Freeze	81					✔			✔	
Prepositions with Rhythm	82			✔					✔	
Same Noise/Different Noise J	109					✔				
Shrinking Animals J	110		✔							
Siren Singing J	111		✔							
Strung Along	88				✔				✔	
Stuff the Can	89			✔				✔		✔
Telebounce Relay	93				✔	✔			✔	
This Is the Way We . . .	95			✔	✔				✔	
Walking the Plank	96								✔	
Word Hopping	100								✔	

J = Jiffies

Guide to Math Readiness Activities

	Page	Measuring	Number Recognition	One-to-One Correspondence	Oral Counting
Back Scrambles	24		✔		
Balloon Matching	28		✔		
Bean Socks	30	✔			
Cotton Ball Blews	36		✔		✔
Do You Hear What I Hear?	38		✔		✔
Flamingo Fandango J	106			✔	✔
Hoppity Different	46		✔		
Hop to It J	107		✔		
Human Bowling Pins	48		✔		
Judge for Yourself	54	✔			
Macrame Writing	57		✔		
Measure and Compare	58	✔			
Memory Coursing	60			✔	
Musical Ball	62		✔		
Name That Time	67		✔		
Number Ball	69		✔	✔	✔
Penny for Your Thoughts	70			✔	✔
Plates of Shapes	74			✔	
Plates of Shapes Revisited	77		✔	✔	✔
Scooterboard Flash	84		✔		
Shopping Spree	86		✔		
Stuff the Can	89			✔	✔
Wheelbarrow Numbers	98		✔	✔	✔

J = Jiffies

Guide to Motor and Sensorimotor Activities

	Page	Balance/Vestibular	Body Awareness	Endurance/Proximal Stability	Motor Planning	Oral Motor	Proprioception	Tactile	Visual Memory	Visual Motor	Visual Perception
Absurd Tug-o-War	19	✔		✔							
Alpha-Ball	21				✔					✔	✔
Animal House	23		✔		✔						
Appliance Alive J	104		✔		✔						
Back Scrambles	24						✔				✔
Balloon Body Parts	26		✔		✔		✔				
Balloon Matching	28						✔	✔			✔
Bean Socks	30		✔		✔				✔		
A Bigger Room C	118		✔	✔			✔				
The Boxer E	114		✔		✔						
Burrito Wrap C	118		✔				✔	✔			
Circle Push C	119		✔	✔			✔				
Clappy Days	32		✔		✔		✔	✔			
Connect the Children	34		✔		✔						✔
Cotton Ball Blews	36			✔		✔			✔		
Echo Clap J	105		✔		✔		✔				
Fishing for an Occupation	39	✔								✔	
Flamingo Fandango J	106	✔	✔		✔						
Hanging Out C	119			✔	✔		✔				
Harvesting Descriptors	41				✔					✔	
Hip, Hip, Hooray E	116		✔		✔						
Hop-Along Letters	43	✔		✔	✔		✔				
Hopping to Feel	44	✔						✔			

C = Calming   E = Excitatory   J = Jiffies

Guide to Motor and Sensorimotor Activities
(continued)

	Page	Balance/Vestibular	Body Awareness	Endurance/Proximal Stability	Motor Planning	Oral Motor	Proprioception	Tactile	Visual Memory	Visual Motor	Visual Perception
Hoppity-Different	46	✔		✔	✔		✔				
Hop to It[J]	107	✔			✔						
Human Bowling Pins	48		✔		✔						✔
Identify Yourself	50				✔					✔	✔
If the Lid Fits . . .	51		✔	✔		✔				✔	
Jet Set Shopping	53		✔	✔	✔						
Judge for Yourself	54		✔		✔						✔
Jump to It[E]	114	✔			✔						
Key Word Stories	56				✔				✔		✔
Logging Time[E]	115	✔		✔			✔				
Macrame Writing	57		✔	✔			✔			✔	
Measure and Compare	58			✔						✔	✔
Memory Coursing	60	✔	✔	✔	✔						
Moving Company[C]	120		✔				✔	✔			
Musical Ball	62		✔	✔					✔		✔
Musical Chair Descriptions	64		✔								
Name and Describe	66		✔		✔						
Name That Time	67		✔								✔
Number Ball	69				✔					✔	✔
One-Person Tug-o-War[C]	120	✔	✔				✔				
Penny for Your Thoughts	70				✔					✔	✔
Pinning with a Song	72		✔		✔					✔	
Plates of Shapes	74	✔		✔						✔	

[C] = Calming   [E] = Excitatory   [J] = Jiffies

continued

Guide to Motor and Sensorimotor Activities

(continued)

	Page	Balance/Vestibular	Body Awareness	Endurance/Proximal Stability	Motor Planning	Oral Motor	Proprioception	Tactile	Visual Memory	Visual Motor	Visual Perception
Plates of Shapes Revisited	77	✔			✔					✔	
Prep-O-Ball	80		✔		✔						
Prepositional Freeze	81		✔		✔						
Prepositions with Rhythm	82		✔		✔						
Rhyme Time	83								✔		
Rhyming Hops ᴶ	109	✔			✔						
Scooterboard Flash	84			✔			✔		✔	✔	✔
Shopping Spree	86	✔		✔			✔		✔		✔
Siren Singing ᴶ	111		✔		✔						
Slap Happy ᴱ	115		✔		✔						
Strung Along	88		✔		✔						
Stuff the Can	89		✔				✔	✔		✔	
Targeting Sounds	91									✔	✔
Telebounce Relay	93	✔		✔	✔		✔				
This Is the Way We . . .	95		✔		✔						
Vocal Play ᴶ	111					✔					
Walking the Plank	96	✔			✔						✔
Wheelbarrow Memory	97		✔	✔	✔		✔	✔			
Wheelbarrow Numbers	98		✔	✔	✔		✔			✔	
Word Hopping	100	✔		✔	✔						
Yea, Friend ᴱ	116		✔		✔						

ᶜ = Calming   ᴱ = Excitatory   ᴶ = Jiffies

Guide to Speech and Language Activities

	Page	Auditory Discrimination	Auditory Memory	Body Language	Comparatives/Superlatives	Linguistic Concepts	Matching	Negation/Exclusion	Oral Motor	Problem Solving	Reasoning	Vocabulary	Word Association
Absurd Tug-o-War	19									✔	✔		✔
Animal House	23			✔			✔					✔	
Appliance Alive ᴶ	104			✔									
Back Scrambles	24									✔	✔		
Balloon Matching	28		✔										
Bean Socks	30									✔			
Clappy Days	32		✔										
Connect the Children	34									✔			
Cotton Ball Blews	36						✔		✔				
Do You Hear What I Hear?	38	✔	✔										
Echo Clap ᴶ	105	✔											
Fishing for an Occupation	39			✔								✔	✔
Flamingo Fandango ᴶ	106			✔									
Harvesting Descriptors	41			✔								✔	✔
Hop-Along Letters	43						✔						
Hoppity Different	46						✔						
Hop to It ᴶ	107						✔						
Human Bowling Pins	48						✔						
I Am Going . . . ᴶ	108		✔										
Identify Yourself	50	✔					✔						
If the Lid Fits . . .	51									✔			
Jet Set Shopping	53							✔				✔	
Judge for Yourself	54	✔			✔								
Key Word Stories	56		✔										✔
Macrame Writing	57									✔			

ᴶ = Jiffies

continued

Guide to Speech and Language Activities

(continued)

	Page	Auditory Discrimination	Auditory Memory	Body Language	Comparatives/Superlatives	Linguistic Concepts	Matching	Negation/Exclusion	Oral Motor	Problem Solving	Reasoning	Vocabulary	Word Association
Measure and Compare	58				✔								
Memory Coursing	60		✔										
Musical Ball	62	✔					✔						
Musical Chair Descriptions	64	✔											
Name That Time	67					✔						✔	
Penny for Your Thoughts	70				✔	✔							
Pinning with a Song	72		✔										
Plates of Shapes	74				✔	✔	✔						
Plates of Shapes Revisited	77					✔							
Prep-O-Ball	80		✔										
Prepositional Freeze	81	✔											
Prepositions with Rhythm	82	✔											
Rhyme Time	83	✔											
Same Noise/Different Noise[J]	109	✔											
Scooterboard Flash	84		✔										
Shopping Spree	86										✔		
Shrinking Animals[J]	110	✔	✔								✔		
Siren Singing[J]	111			✔									
Stuff the Can	89									✔			
Telebounce Relay	93		✔										
This Is the Way We . . .	95			✔									
Vocal Play[J]	111								✔				
Walking the Plank	96									✔			
Wheelbarrow Memory	97	✔			✔								
Wheelbarrow Numbers	98						✔						

[J] = Jiffies

ACTIVITIES

Absurd Tug-o-War

*Children practice recognizing verbal absurdities
and correcting them in complete sentences
during a tug-o-war.*

Skill Areas: listening; sentence usage; balance; endurance; problem solving; reasoning; word association

Time Required: 20-30 minutes

Materials
15-foot rope
masking tape
marker

Entry Level
With masking tape, make two parallel lines on the floor about three feet apart. Mark the center of the rope with a heavy line. Divide the class into two teams. The two teams line up facing each other behind the tape lines. On your signal, both teams pull on the rope until one team succeeds in pulling the center of the rope over its line.

Present the first child on the winning team with a sentence. Give a choice for one of the words in the sentence, one of which makes sense and one of which is absurd. (For example, "Tobias wore his [shoes or gloves] on his hands.") The child repeats the sentence using the word that makes sense. (See Sample Absurd Sentences at the end of this activity.)

Ask the first child on the losing team to make up a sentence using the other word. Team members may consult, if needed. Both the leading children move to the end of their lines, and the tug-o-war resumes.

continued

Intermediate Level

Read the first child on the winning team an absurd sentence. The child identifies what is wrong with the sentence. Then the first child on the losing team changes the sentence so that it makes sense.

Advanced Level

Provide the first child on the winning team with a key word (for example, "snowing"). The child may choose whether to form an absurd sentence or a sensible sentence using the key word. The child on the losing team then provides the other sentence.

Sample Absurd Sentences for Entry Level

- It was snowing outside, so Shakena put on her [bathing suit or snow suit].
- Mom said, "Go milk the [horse or cow]."
- We drove the [car or boat] on the street.
- Sol turned off the light so he could [sleep or read].

Alpha-Ball

*Children practice reciting the letters of the alphabet
or naming letters while playing a ball game.*

Skill Areas: letter recognition; phonics (advanced); motor planning; visual motor; visual perception

Time Required: 20-30 minutes

Materials

    playground or medium-sized ball
    letter flash cards (*intermediate and advanced levels*)

Entry Level

    The children stand in two lines facing each other. Starting at one end, the children hand off the ball back and forth down the lines until it reaches the other end. As each child receives the ball, he or she recites a letter of the alphabet (in order). You can either have all the children recite the alphabet in unison with each pass of the ball, or have only the child who receives the ball recite the letter.

continued

Intermediate Level

The children stand in two lines and pass the ball as in the entry level. Instead of reciting the alphabet, however, the children name letters written on flash cards. As each child receives the ball, hold up a flash card and have the child name the letter.

If a child names a letter incorrectly, respond with tactful feedback that the response was incorrect. (For example, "That's close" or "Let's see what Chyvonn says.") The ball is passed to the next child, who tries to name the same letter. The children continue to pass the ball and try to name the same letter until one child gives the correct answer. Then, the ball is returned to the child who originally missed the letter and it is passed down the lines until all the children who missed that letter have had an opportunity to name it correctly. Continue the game showing a new letter flash card.

Advanced Level

Play the game as described in the intermediate level. However, the children make the sound of the letter on the flash card instead of naming it. You might wish to select letters carefully for this activity to avoid letters that have several possible sounds.

Animal House

Children pantomime and vocalize their interpretations of a variety of animals and categorize the animals.

Skill Areas: inferences; object classification; sentence usage; body awareness; motor planning; body language; negation; vocabulary

Time Required: 30 minutes

Materials

3 large pictures of a house, barn or farm, and zoo—each attached to a box, bag, or cardboard easel (The children can draw these pictures ahead of time.)

smaller pictures of animals that live in these settings

Entry Level

Arrange the three settings where animals live so that all children can see them and access them. Make sure all the children recognize what the settings are. Show an animal card to the children and ask them to move as they imagine this animal would move.

Tell the children in which setting the animal lives and why the animal lives there. Place the animal card in the appropriate setting or have one of the children do so.

Intermediate Level

Hold up an animal card and ask one or all of the children to imitate the animal's movement and, if appropriate, the sound the animal makes. Moving as the animal does, one child takes the picture to the setting where the animal lives and places it there.

Advanced Level

Conduct the activity as described for the intermediate level. However, after placing the animal in its correct setting, have the child say why the animal would *not* belong in the other two settings.

Back Scrambles

Reading Readiness
Math Readiness

*Children duplicate on a chalkboard simple shapes,
numbers, or letters drawn on their backs.*

Skill Areas: directionality/prepositions; letter, shape, and number recognition;
patterns/sequencing; tactile; visual perception; problem solving; reasoning

Time Required: 30-40 minutes

Materials
flash cards or index cards
chalkboard space for ¹/₂ of the number of children (or paper taped to the
wall)
writing implements for chalkboard/paper

Entry Level
Draw two or three different shapes on each index card.

The children pair up. The first child (the drawee) stands facing the chalkboard
or paper, and the second child (the drawer) faces the first child's back. The
drawer will draw shapes on the drawee's back.

The drawer "prepares" the drawee's back by stroking (with moderate force) once in each of the following directions. (Have all children perform these actions simultaneously while they repeat them aloud. Depending upon the levels of your students, not all directions will be appropriate.)

left to right	bottom to top
top to bottom	top left to bottom right
top right to bottom left	right to left
up	down

As the drawer is rubbing the drawee's back, the drawee duplicates the movements on the chalkboard or paper while repeating the drawer's directions aloud.

Now hold up a flash card with a sequence of two or three shapes drawn on it. Using one finger, the drawer draws the first shape on the drawee's back, after which the drawee duplicates that shape on the chalkboard or paper. When the drawee has correctly duplicated the first shape, the drawer draws the second shape.

A few children may have trouble drawing on the drawee's back. Because all the children will be drawing the same shape, you can encourage peers to assist one another or have an aide assist the child. If need be, stand at the front of the room (with your back to the drawer) and draw the target shape in the air for the drawer to model.

Have the drawer and drawee exchange places, then continue the activity with a new set of shape sequence cards.

Intermediate Level

Draw two or three numbers on each card. Numbers should not be in numerical order (ex: 4 3 5). Conduct the activity as described for the entry level. After the drawee has correctly duplicated the numbers on the board, have the pair of children work together to rearrange the numbers in numerical order (ex: 4 3 5 becomes 3 4 5).

Advanced Level

Write a scrambled two- or three-letter word on each card. Use familiar sight words or children's names. Write the unscrambled words on a matching set of cards and post within easy view of the children.

Give each drawer a card with a scrambled word on it. The drawer writes one letter at a time on the drawee's back. Make sure the children draw large letters (at least 10 inches high). When the drawee has correctly duplicated all the letters in the scrambled word on the chalkboard, the pair of children works as a team to match the scrambled letters to the correct unscrambled word.

Balloon Body Parts

Children place balloons on designated body parts.

Skill Areas: body part identification; following directions; body awareness; motor planning; tactile

Time Required: 30 minutes

Materials
1 balloon per child

Entry Level
Call out a body part and have the students hold their balloons over that body part (or rub the balloon on the body part until static electricity causes it to stick). The children name the body part in unison.

Intermediate Level
Place the balloons at a distance from the children. Call out a mode of loco-motion and a body part. (For example, "I want you to crab walk to the balloons and place a balloon on your shoulder.") The children move toward the balloons in the manner you indicated. When they reach the balloons, each child places a balloon on the designated body part. To increase the complexity of the directions, you can instruct each child to pick up a balloon of a particular color.

Advanced Level
For the advanced level, the children work in pairs. Direct each pair of children to move to the balloons in a certain manner and to return holding a balloon between them with a particular body part. For example, you might say, "Hop to the balloon pile and use your elbows to hold the balloon." The pair will hop to the pile. They each use one elbow to hold a balloon between them, then try to hop back together without losing the balloon.

Balloon Body Parts

Balloon Matching

*Children use balloons with shapes,
numbers, or letters written on them to
recreate a sequence of shapes, numbers,
or letters written on the chalkboard.*

Skill Areas: color, letter, shape, and number recognition; patterns/sequencing; tactile; visual and auditory memory; visual perception

Time Required: 30 minutes

Materials
  multicolored balloons
  chalkboard and colored chalk
  sequence cards with 2 to 5 colors, shapes, letters, or numbers on them

Entry Level
  Draw nothing on one set of balloons; for the second set, draw one shape on each balloon. Prepare one set of sequence cards showing sequences of two to five colors and a second set of sequence cards showing sequences of two to five shapes. Make sure you have enough balloons of the correct colors to duplicate all the sequences.

  Divide the class into groups that correspond to the length of the sequences you will present (for example, three children per group for a three-item sequence). Each group of children stands in a line. Present a sequence of colors to the children by drawing it on the board with colored chalk or showing a large sequence card. Each child in the line takes a balloon so that together they duplicate the sequence in the correct order. While standing with their backs to the chalkboard, the children may hold the balloons in front of them or stick the balloons to their chests using static electricity.

  When the children can successfully duplicate color sequences, introduce the balloons with shapes on them. Have children copy sequences of shapes in the same manner.

Intermediate Level

Prepare a set of sequence cards showing sequences of two to five numbers. Draw a number on each balloon. Make sure you have enough balloons with the correct numbers to duplicate all the sequences.

Hold up a sequence card showing a series of numbers. Allow the students to view the card for 5-10 seconds, reciting the sequence of numbers aloud as they view the card. Then they use the balloons to duplicate the sequence of numbers from memory.

Advanced Level

Use balloons with letters written on them. Show a flash card containing a short word or sequence of three to five random letters. Allow the children to view the card for 5-10 seconds, but don't allow them to rehearse the sequence aloud. Then have them use the balloons as before to copy the sequence of letters. For a higher functioning class, you may wish to use some of the children's names.

Bean Socks

Children make beanbags out of socks.
These "bean socks" are then used for a variety of
games targeting different concepts.

Skill Areas: directionality/prepositions; body part identification; descriptor use; prediction; measuring; body awareness; motor planning (*advanced level*); visual motor; problem solving

Time Required: 30 minutes to make bean socks; 20-30 minutes for activities

Materials
1 sock (free of holes) per child
1 cup filling per child; use a variety of fillings: lentils, mixed beans, pop-
    corn, split peas
rubber bands
measuring cups
scale

Making the Bean Socks
Each child receives a sock and measures one cup of filling for it. If two or more fillings are available, children can compare the densities and weights of the different filling materials. You can also discuss what food groups the fillings belong in, how and where they are grown, and how they are harvested and prepared.

After the socks are filled, the opening is either knotted or closed securely with rubber bands.

Entry Level
During simple catching and throwing games, children try to guess which filling is inside of each sock. Have the children practice one- and two-handed catching while standing, then while lying on their stomachs, kneeling, or standing on one foot.

Have the children throw the bean socks at targets while standing, lying, kneeling, or standing on one foot.

Intermediate Level

The children form a circle with each child facing the back of the next child in the circle. Give every other child a bean sock.

Call out the direction in which the children must pass their bean socks ("in front of you" or "behind you"). For example, when you say "behind," everyone with a bean sock passes it to the person behind him or her. The children continue passing the bean socks in the direction specified while you periodically call out different ways they should pass the socks. Methods of passing include these:

- over your head, over your shoulder

- under your leg, under your arm

- around your arm, around your waist, around your neck

Once the children understand the various ways of passing the bean socks, increase the complexity of the activity. You might ask them to pass the bean socks at different speeds or to march around the circle (so that the circle rotates) while they pass the bean socks. Another interesting alternative is to have them walk on their knees around the circle while passing the bean socks.

Advanced Level

Give each child a bean sock. Without naming specific body parts, direct the children to place their bean socks on different areas of their bodies and move around the circle. The children have to decide how they can follow your direction. Here are some examples:

- "Move with a bean sock on top of your body." (Children could walk with the bean socks on their heads.)

- "Move with a bean sock on the bottom of your body." (Children could balance the bean socks on their ankles or the tops of their feet and walk or hop around the circle.)

- "Move with a bean sock on the back of your body." (Children could crawl on all fours with the bean socks on their backs.)

- "Move with a bean sock on the front of your body." (Children could crab walk balancing the bean socks on their stomachs.)

After allowing the children to problem solve on their own for a time, it is fine to demonstrate your solutions to them.

Clappy Days

Children practice sequencing the days of the week.
This activity will familiarize children with reciting
and recognizing the days of the week.

Skill Areas: word/name recognition; descriptor use; time concepts; body awareness; motor planning; proprioception; tactile; auditory memory

Time Required: 20-30 minutes

Materials
> 7 pieces of paper (8½" x 11" or larger), each with one day of the week written on it
> 7 index cards, each with one day of the week written on it
> 1 paper bag

Entry Level
Place the index cards in the paper bag. Have seven children line up facing the class, each holding a paper with a day of the week written on it. Have them line up in the order of the days of the week, beginning with Sunday and ending with Saturday.

A child selects an index card from the bag. Read the day of the week that is on the card. You and the children recite the days of the week in unison, clapping once for each day. When the class reaches the day that was on the index card, the child holding that day raises the card overhead as the chanters give an extra loud clap. Continue reciting the remaining days of the week, clapping once for each day.

Intermediate Level
Conduct the activity as described in the entry level, but when a child selects an index card, ask what day comes after the one on the card. (For example, if the card reads "Tuesday," ask, "What day comes after Tuesday?") If the child cannot answer, ask the class to recite the sequence of days as in the entry level. Instruct the child to listen for the correct answer.

Advanced Level

Conduct the activity in the same manner as the intermediate level. Ask the child who selects the index card to name the days that come *before* and *after* the day on the card.

To help with word recognition, ask the children in line to hold up the day before and the day after the target day as the children recite the days of the week while clapping.

Connect the Children

*Children practice drawing shapes while they develop
body and spatial awareness.*

Skill Areas: shape recognition; prediction; body awareness; motor planning;
visual perception; problem solving

Time Required: 30 minutes

Materials
chalkboard and chalk
chalk and chalkboard space or paper and pencil or crayon for each child
    (*entry level*)
10 pieces of string, each roughly 3 yards long (*intermediate level*)

Entry Level
Draw a dotted outline of a shape on the chalkboard. For example, draw a
dotted square with eight dots: one dot in each corner and one dot in the
middle of each side of the square.

Working individually or in groups, the children determine what shape would
result from connecting the dots and draw that shape on the paper or chalkboard. Connect the dots on your outline and have the class name the resulting shape. Did all the children draw the correct shape?

Intermediate Level

Clear an open area in the classroom. Divide the children into groups of between four and nine. Draw a dotted outline on the board using three to eight dots (there should be one fewer dots than the number of children).

Have each group of children create a "living outline" of the shape, with each child representing a dot. The remaining child, who doesn't form part of the outline, takes a length of string and walks around the outline using the string to connect the "dots." (The children who are dots take hold of the string to keep it in place.) When the child has rounded the perimeter, all the children will be connected to form a shape.

Connect the dots on the chalkboard so the children can see whether their shape is correct.

Advanced Level

Using the dots on the chalkboard as a guide, children form themselves into the shape which would be apparent if the dots were connected. The children should hold hands to create a closed shape. At this level, the string is not used as a visual cue.

Cotton Ball Blews

> Reading Readiness
> Math Readiness

*Children use straws to blow cotton balls
to specified destinations.*

Skill Areas: color and number recognition (*entry level*); oral counting; oral motor; proximal stability; visual motor; matching

Time Required: 10-20 minutes

Materials
straw for each child
cotton balls, dyed various colors or colored with markers
sheets of construction paper in matching colors (8½" x 11" or larger)
marker
masking tape
timer or stopwatch (*intermediate level*)

Entry Level
Clear an area of the room. Tape the construction paper sheets at different locations around the area.

Divide the children into groups and assign each group a different color. Give each child a straw.

Pile all the cotton balls in the center of the floor and position the children around the cotton balls. Each group of children tries to be the first to blow all the cotton balls of their assigned color to the matching sheet of paper.

Repeat the game, assigning each group a different color. Continue until the children have rotated through all the colors.

Intermediate Level
Pile all the colored cotton balls in the center of the room and assign each group a color as before. Give the children a time limit (30-40 seconds, or longer if needed) within which they must blow as many cotton balls of their assigned color as they can to their paper. When you call time, each group counts how many cotton balls are on its paper; the group with the most wins.

Advanced Level

Pile the cotton balls in the center of the room. Write a number on each of the pieces of paper taped around the room. Each group is assigned a piece of paper and must blow the corresponding number of cotton balls to that paper. (The cotton balls must stay on the paper.)

One at a time, each group counts the number of cotton balls on its piece of paper aloud. The other children confirm whether the correct number of cotton balls is on the sheet. Continue the game until the groups have rotated through all the numbers.

Do You Hear What I Hear?

> Reading Readiness
> Language and Listening
> Math Readiness

*Without using their vision, children listen
to a sequence of sounds then attempt to
duplicate the sequence.*

Skill Areas: patterns/sequencing; listening; number recognition; oral
counting; auditory discrimination; auditory memory

Time Required: 30-40 minutes

Materials
variety of noisemakers
number flash cards (one per child)

Entry Level
Demonstrate the noisemakers and give the children an opportunity to try each
one. Give each child a flash card with a different number on it. Then have the
children turn their backs to you and close their eyes so they cannot see you
using the noisemakers. Make a noise with one of the noisemakers, then have
the children open their eyes and turn around. Call out a number at random.
The child holding that number comes forward and tries to duplicate the noise
you made. The remaining children judge whether the sound was correct.

Intermediate Level
Conduct the activity as in the entry level but make two or three sounds while
the children's backs are turned. Call out a number and have the child with that
number try to duplicate the sequence of sounds you made.

Advanced Level
Conduct the activity as in the intermediate level, but make the sequences more
complex: make each noise in the sequence a different number of times. Have
the children duplicate both the correct number of repetitions and the correct
sequence of noisemakers.

Fishing for an Occupation

*Children use gross motor and eye-hand coordination
skills as they pantomime a variety of occupations.*

Skill Areas: descriptor use; inferences; sentence usage; balance; visual motor;
body language; vocabulary; word association

Time Required: 30 minutes

Materials
two matching sets of occupation pictures
paper clips
a fishing pole made of dowel or stiff cardboard
string
horseshoe magnet

Attach a paper clip to each card in one set of occupation pictures.
Tie the string to one end of the fishing pole, then tie the magnet
to the end of the string.

Entry Level
Name and review the occupation pictures with the children. Place the paper-
clipped set of pictures face-up in a pile (the "fishing hole") 10 to 12 feet away
from the children. Keep the matching set of pictures.

Show a picture of an occupation to the children and have one child hop to
the fishing hole to find the match. On reaching the fishing hole, the child lies
prone and uses the fishing pole to "fish out" the matching picture. After catching this "fish," the child names the occupation and briefly describes it.

Intermediate Level
Select a picture and, without showing it to the children, describe the setting
and tools associated with this occupation. The first child hops to the fishing
hole, catches the picture that he or she believes to be the occupation you
described, and asks the rest of the class whether this is the right picture. If
the child has selected the wrong picture, then another child takes a turn and
tries to select the correct one. The child hops back to the line, and the next
child takes a turn.

continued

Advanced Level

One child stands next to the fishing hole and acts out one of the pictured occupations. The first child in line hops to the fishing hole and fishes out the corresponding occupation. The rest of the class passes judgment on the correctness of the catch. Together the fisher and the pantomimer name and describe the occupation.

Variations: Have the children move to the fishing hole in a variety of ways, including these:

- crab walking
- walking backwards
- jumping
- heel walking
- seal walking
- walking or jumping sideways

Have the children "fish out" the correct picture in a variety of positions:

- sitting cross-legged
- kneeling
- lying on one side
- side sitting
- stooping

Harvesting Descriptors

*Children pantomime a gardening activity and use
pictures of fruits and vegetables cut from magazines
in identification and classification tasks.*

Skill Areas: color recognition (*entry level*); descriptor use; object
classification; motor planning; visual motor; body language; vocabulary;
word association

Time Required: 20-30 minutes

Materials
several pairs of scissors
glue
posterboard
magazines containing pictures of fruits and vegetables

Entry Level
Discuss with the class the process and vocabulary associated with growing
plants—for example, planting, watering, weeding, harvesting, vines, roots,
trees, and so on. Children pantomime the process of growing plants, including planting the seed, hoeing the weeds, watering the plants, and harvesting
or pulling up the grown plant.

Give the children scissors and a supply of magazines. Assign each child or
group of children to search for fruits and vegetables of a given color. (You can
decide on the number of different colors to include.) For example, if the color
is orange, the child could search for oranges, pumpkins, carrots, and squash.

Help the children mount all the pictures of a given color on one piece of
posterboard to make a collage. Make a separate collage for each color. Have
the class name all the foods on the collages.

continued

Intermediate Level

Begin by introducing relevant vocabulary and pantomiming the process of growing plants, as described in the entry level. Give each child or group of children scissors and a supply of magazines. Assign the children to search either for kinds of fruit or for vegetables.

When the children have cut out several pictures, have them mount the vegetables on one piece of posterboard and the fruits on another piece to make two collages. Display the collages to the class. Ask questions similar to the following:

- Do you cook this food? How do you cook it?

- Can you buy this food in a can at the grocery store?

- Do you eat this food with a fork, a spoon, or your fingers?

You might bring in some exotic fruits and vegetables, or ask the children to bring in some, for a "show and tell" session. If appropriate, allow the children to try these unfamiliar foods.

Advanced Level

Begin by introducing relevant vocabulary and pantomiming the process of growing plants, as described in the entry level. Display either the entry level or intermediate level collages, and ask the children to describe the fruits and vegetables. For example:

- On what type of plant does this fruit (vegetable) grow?

- Could you grow the plant around here? Why or why not?

- Do you have to peel this fruit (vegetable) before you eat it?

- Is it fuzzy? Smooth? Juicy? Hard? Soft?

Hop-Along Letters

Children develop letter recognition and sound recognition skills while they use a hopping ball.

Skill Areas: letter recognition; phonics; balance; endurance/proximal stability; motor planning; proprioception; matching

Time Required: 20-30 minutes

Materials
2 hopping balls such as Hoppity-Hop Balls®
3 identical sets of letter flash cards

Entry Level
Divide the children into two lines and place one pile of letters opposite each line of children at a distance of roughly 10 to 12 feet. Give the first child in each line a hopping ball, and show each child a different letter flash card. The children hop to their respective letter piles, find the matching letter cards, and hop back. Each child shows the letter card to the other children in line. Everyone names the letter and draws it in the air. Repeat until every child has had a turn.

Intermediate Level
Tell each child a different letter (rather than showing flash cards). Have the children hop to retrieve the matching cards as before. However, when each child shows the letter, all the children in line who have that letter in their names raise their hands.

Advanced Level
Perform the activity in the same manner as the intermediate level, but identify the letter by sound rather than by name. When each child returns to the line with the letter, ask the other children in line to provide a word that starts with that sound.

Hopping to Feel

*Teams hop to bags of objects and compete
to identify a common object they cannot see by
describing and feeling it.*

Skill Areas: same/different; descriptor use; listening; object classification; sentence usage; balance; tactile

Time Required: 30 minutes

Materials
2 hopping balls such as Hoppity Hop Balls®
paper bag
pairs of similar objects, such as the following:

small and large paper clips	pen and pencil
crayon and marker	plastic and metal spoons
plastic and metal forks	balls of 2 different sizes and textures
2 different sized balloons (deflated)	

Entry Level
Familiarize the children with the items while dividing the class into two teams: place all the items in one bag. Each child draws an item from the bag and looks for the child who drew a similar item. These two children are then on opposite teams. If appropriate, ask the pairs of children how their items are similar and different (for example, they are both forks, but one is metal and the other is plastic).

Return all the items to the paper bag. The teams line up at the opposite end of the room from the paper bag. The first two children in line get on the hopping balls. Tell these children which pair of objects they are to find in the bag. The two children race on the hopping balls to the bag. *Without looking,* they both simultaneously feel in the bag for the objects.

Once they have found the objects, the children hold them up. Each child gives a sentence describing the function or inherent qualities of the pair of objects. For example, with reference to a fork, the children might say: "You use it for eating" and "It has sharp points."

Both objects are returned to the bag. The children hop back to their respective lines, and the process is repeated with the next children in line.

Intermediate Level

Instead of naming the objects the pair of children are to find, describe them by function. For example, "Find the things you use for eating." The children hop on their balls to the bag and feel for the objects as before. After they have the objects, one child then describes one way in which the two items are alike, and the other child describes how they are different.

Advanced Level

The first pair of children races to the paper bag on the hopping balls. The first child to reach the bag chooses an item from it, *without* letting the second child see it. The first child describes the item to the second child who must, again without looking, find the matching item. The entire class makes up a sentence that describes both items.

Hoppity Different

Reading Readiness
Language and Listening
Math Readiness

Children travel on hopping balls while they practice comparison and contrast skills.

Skill Areas: letter and number recognition; same/different; descriptor use; sentence usage; balance; endurance/proximal stability; motor planning; proprioception; matching

Time Required: 30-35 minutes

Materials

2 hopping balls such as Hoppity Hop Balls®
pairs of similar but not identical objects (for example, plastic and metal spoons)
flash cards with numbers or letters written on them (Make 4 cards for each number or letter, and make the number of different numbers or letters equal to ½ the number of children.)
paper bag

Entry Level

Place two sets of number or letter cards in the paper bag. Each child selects a card from the bag. The children compare their cards, and the children who have matching cards become partners for the activity.

In easy view of the children, arrange the sets of paired objects in a row at the other end of the room. Label each pair of objects with a number or letter card to match the cards the children have.

Hold up a number or letter flash card. The two children who have that number or letter get on the hopping balls; both hop to the pair of objects labeled with the matching number or letter. One child describes one thing that is different about the two objects; the other child describes one way in which they are the same.

Intermediate Level

Conduct the activity as in the entry level, but instead of holding up a flash card, call a number or letter aloud.

Advanced Level

Conduct the activity as described in the intermediate level. However, when the pair of children reaches the objects, each gives *two* ways in which the objects are alike or different. If necessary, the children may ask their classmates for help.

Human Bowling Pins

Children play an adapted version of bowling to learn shapes and practice sequencing.

Skill Areas: letter, number, and shape recognition; patterns/sequencing; body awareness; motor planning; visual perception; matching

Time Required: 30 minutes

Materials

1 playground ball

various shapes, letters, or numbers cut out of construction paper

safety pins

flash cards showing sequences of shapes, letters, or numbers (Gear the length of the sequences to the skill of the class.)

Entry Level

Children volunteer to wear one of the paper shapes. The remaining children form a circle around the children who are wearing shapes. The shape-wearing children standing inside the circle close their eyes while you show the children who are forming the circle a card with a sequence of shapes.

The children forming the circle must "bowl" (roll the ball underhand) to hit the children who are wearing the corresponding shapes. They have to target the children in the sequence shown on the flash card. The children who are hit by the ball remove themselves from within the circle and line up in the order they were hit to duplicate the sequence on the flash card. Even if the wrong child is hit, that child leaves the circle and lines up in the sequence. When all the children have been tagged out, hold up the flash card again. The entire class checks to see whether the line of children matches the sequence on the card.

It is very important to have strict rules in this game to prevent any of the children from getting hurt. The children in the circle must roll the ball underhand, rather than throwing it. They must aim for the targeted child's legs or feet. Any child who throws with excessive force or hits another child above the waist must sit out for the remainder of the game.

Intermediate Level

Conduct the activity as in the entry level but with sequences of numbers rather than shapes.

Advanced Level

Conduct the activity as in the entry level but with simple three-letter words or names of class members rather than shapes.

Identify Yourself

*Children practice letter and name
recognition while marching in a circle.*

Skill Areas: letter and word/name recognition; motor planning; visual motor; visual perception; auditory discrimination; matching

Time Required: 30 minutes

Materials
large cards (or sheets of paper) with a different letter on each one
alphabet line (strip showing the printed alphabet) within children's reach on the wall *or* chalk and chalkboard
flash cards showing 3- or 4-letter words *or* chalkboard (*intermediate level*)
paper grocery bags, each with eyeholes cut out and a different large letter written on it (*advanced level*)

Entry Level
Each child is given a letter card containing a letter that is in his or her first name. The children march around in a circle holding their cards. Call out a letter. The child holding that letter card holds it up, marches to the chalkboard, and either finds it on the alphabet line or writes it (if appropriate) on the chalkboard. In unison, the class repeats the letter that the child has written. The child marches back to the circle. Repeat the process with another letter.

Intermediate Level
As the children march in a circle holding their letter cards, hold up a flash card with a word on it. The children who are carrying letters in that word hold up their letter cards. In unison, the class repeats the letters that are held up and verifies that they are in the word.

Advanced Level
All children but one receive grocery bags with letters on them to wear on their heads. These children form a circle and march in place. The child who does not have a grocery bag stands in the center of the circle. Call out a letter and ask the child inside the circle to find the child wearing the bag with that letter. The child in the center exchanges places with that child, and the activity continues.

If the Lid Fits . . .

Children have a wheelbarrow race to pair lids with the corresponding containers.

Skill Areas: descriptor use (*advanced level*); inferences; prediction; sentence usage; endurance/proximal stability; motor planning; proprioception; visual motor; problem solving

Time Required: 30-45 minutes

Materials

10 or more unbreakable jars or containers in various sizes with matching lids

blindfolds (*advanced level*)

Entry Level

Remove the lids from the containers. Place the containers and lids in two separate piles 10 or 12 feet from the children. Divide the class into two teams. Within each team, have the children pair up. The first pair of children on each team forms a two-person wheelbarrow. (That is, one child holds the second child's ankles while the second child walks on his or her hands.) The pairs of children move in this way to the pile of jars, where each pair selects a container. They then move to the pile of lids, where each pair decides (by consensus) which lid fits the container (choices should be fairly obvious).

Each pair has one chance to select the lid that fits by visual inspection (without trying any of the lids to see if they fit). If the lid does not fit the container, both items are returned to their respective piles, and the next pair of children takes a turn. If the lid fits, both the lid and container are removed from the piles.

When introducing this game, you may wish to have the teams take turns so that only one pair of children is in motion at a time. As the children become familiar with the activity, you can have the teams race one another.

continued

Intermediate Level

Increase the number of lids and containers. You could also select lids that are more similar in size and shape. Rather than the two children in the wheelbarrow deciding at the pile which lid will fit the container, the entire team must agree from a distance which lid fits (forcing them to describe the lids). No lids may be tried on the container until everyone agrees on the choice.

Advanced Level

Once the wheelbarrow pair reaches the pile of containers, they are both blindfolded. Their team must verbally guide them to the correct container and lid. (This is best done only one team at a time.) Perhaps one child can be asked to select the container while the other selects the lid (both blindfolded). The team decides whether the lid will fit the container and, if not, why not. For example, "The lid is too big" or "You need a round lid, not a square one." The two children remove their blindfolds and test whether the lid fits the container.

Jet Set Shopping

*Using scooterboards, children develop language skills
as they play "airport."*

Skill Areas: object classification; body awareness; endurance; motor
planning; exclusion; vocabulary

Time Required: 30-40 minutes

Materials
2 scooterboards
2 bags containing a variety of pictures representing locations within the
community (ex: a can of food representing a grocery; an envelope
representing a post office)

Entry Level
Set up two intersecting paths which the "airplanes" (scooterboards) can use
as runways. Place a bag filled with pictures at the end of each runway. Have
the children form two teams, then pair up within their teams. Each team lines
up at the end of a runway. One member of the pair lies prone on the scooter
with legs straight. The second child takes hold of the first child's ankles and
pushes the child as shown in the illustration for "Shopping Spree" (page 87).
The children on the scooterboards are piloted down their respective runways
with strict reminders to pass each other at the intersection *without* colliding.
If appropriate, designate a child to act as "air traffic controller" to prevent
collisions.

When the pair of children reaches the bag, one child reaches in and, without
looking, selects a picture. The other child states where in the community the
pictured object could be found. (ex: "A can of food is found at the grocery
store.") The children then switch positions and pilot back to their "hangar."
Repeat until all the children have had a turn.

Intermediate Level
Conduct the activity as in the entry level. However, after naming the place where
the pictured item can be found, the children name two additional items found
in the same location.

Advanced Level
Perform in the same manner as the intermediate level. However, in addition
to naming two items found in the pictured location, have the children also
name one item that would *not* be found in that location.

Judge for Yourself

*Children practice visually measuring distances and
the concept of closer (nearer).*

Skill Areas: descriptor use; listening; prediction; measuring; body
awareness; motor planning; visual perception; auditory discrimination;
comparatives/superlatives

Time Required: 30 minutes

Materials
ruler
string or yarn
scissors
noisemaker (rhythm instrument, whistle, or bell)
space large enough for all children to walk in; can be bounded by chairs,
rope, or masking tape

Entry Level
Have each child measure a piece of string or yarn (the same or different
lengths, depending on the concept you wish to teach). Each child cuts the
designated length of string and carries it throughout the activity.

Establish the area within which the children will walk. If you are targeting
measurement skills, you might ask the children how much room they think
they will need so they can walk without bumping into one another. If appropriate, have them measure the boundary lines of the area.

While you maintain a steady rhythm with the noisemaker, the children walk
within the designated area. When you stop the rhythm—perhaps also blowing a whistle as a signal to stop—the children immediately freeze.

When the children stop, ask one child, "Who is closest to you and who is
farthest from you?" Ask that child to predict whether the string will reach to
the closest and farthest child. You may wish to have the rest of the class give
input regarding the child's predictions. Try out their predictions.

Intermediate Level

When the children stop, ask a specific child a question regarding the relative distances of two other students. For example, "Sally, who is closer to you, Lateisha or Bob?" After the child guesses, have another child measure the two distances to confirm or refute the child's answer.

Advanced Level

After the children stop, ask one of the students to visually compare the length of his or her string against the distance between two classmates. For example, "Juan, is the distance between Marty and Kay longer, shorter, or about the same as your piece of string?" After Juan has made his decision, the entire class can offer their input. Juan then measures the distance with his string.

Key Word Stories

*Children practice describing or
acting out items within particular categories.*

Skill Areas: descriptor use; inferences; sentence usage; motor planning; visual and auditory memory; visual perception; body language; word association

Time Required: 15-40 minutes

Materials

pictures in two different categories, each picture mounted on a separate index card

2 paper bags

Selecting categories: Select two categories that relate to a common theme. For example, if the topic is the month of March, two possible categories might be items relating to St. Patrick's day and items relating to kite flying.

St. Patrick's Day: green clothing, shamrock, pot of gold, leprechaun, rainbow, St. Patrick, pinching, Ireland

Kite flying: string, windy weather, trees, kite, kite tail, running, electrical wires, park

Entry Level

Divide the children into two teams. Give each team a paper bag with one of the categories of pictures in it. One child on the first team draws a picture from the bag. The child makes up a short sentence using the word depicted on the picture. Then a child on the other team takes a turn. The game continues until all the pictures have been removed from both the bags.

Intermediate Level

A child on the first team draws a picture out of the bag then acts out or describes the picture to the children on the other team. The children on the other team try to guess what the picture is. The teams take turns acting out and guessing the pictures until both bags are empty.

Advanced Level

After both teams have finished guessing each other's pictures, the pictures are returned to the paper bags. Each team now tries to recall and name all the pictures presented by the other team.

Macrame Writing

*Children use macrame cords
to trace shapes, letters, words, or numbers.*

Skill Areas: directionality/prepositions; letter, number, or word/name recognition; body awareness; motor planning; tactile; visual motor; problem solving

Time Required: 15-30 minutes

Materials

for each child, 2 to 2½ feet of macrame cord (½" or less in diameter)

shapes, letters, numbers, or words, each written on an 8½" x 11" sheet of paper or posterboard (one per child)

alphabet line or alphabet written on chalkboard (*optional*)

Entry Level

Give each child a macrame cord. Have the children "warm up" with a brief isometric exercise that provides tactile and proprioceptive input. Each child grabs the ends of the cord, one end in each hand. Holding the ends of the rope, the child pulls his or her hands apart, as if trying to stretch the cord.

Give each child a shape, number, or letter drawn on a piece of paper or posterboard. The children place their cords over the figure on the posterboard, so that the cord traces the outline of the figure. Have the children lay down the cord in the sequence they would follow to write a well-formed shape, letter, or number.

Once all the children have finished and you have checked their work, have them trade papers and do the activity again.

Intermediate Level

Ask the children to form their macrame cords into a shape, letter, or number *without* giving them a written model to trace. The children may look for the letter on the alphabet line if they need a model. If they are having difficulty, draw a model on the chalkboard.

Advanced Level

Write down on a chalkboard or flash card a familiar sight word or a child's name. Have a group of children form the word, with each child making one of the letters in it.

Measure and Compare

Children practice measuring and comparing sizes using the descriptors "short," "tall," "same," and "different."

Skill Areas: same/different; descriptor use; prediction; measuring; proximal stability; visual motor; visual perception; comparatives/superlatives

Time Required: 20-30 minutes

Materials

1 pair of scissors for each child
index cards with a single number
   from 1-4 written on each
   (one per child)

paper bag
rulers
pencils
construction paper

Entry Level

Place the index cards in the bag. The children work in pairs; each pair should have a pair of scissors, a ruler, a pencil, and a sheet of construction paper. Without looking, each child in the pair selects an index card from the paper bag. The pair of children lies on the floor with the paper placed horizontally in front of them. (Make sure the paper is on a hard surface.) The two children assist each other in manipulating the ruler, measuring the paper, drawing, and cutting two strips of paper that are the designated numbers of inches high (1", 2", 3", or 4"). If necessary, highlight the inch numbers on the ruler.

Each child should now have one strip (the two children in each pair may have strips of different heights). After cutting their strips, the children write a number on each strip indicating how high it is. (For example, a 1 would be written on a 1-inch strip.)

Intermediate Level

Introduce the concepts "short," "shorter," "same," and "different." Have each pair of children compare their strips.

Advanced Level

Introduce the concepts "tall," "taller," and "tallest." Ask the pairs of children to find objects in the room which are "taller" than their strips of paper. Depending on your children's abilities, you can ask them to find objects in the room that are shorter than, taller than, the same height as, or a different height than each child's strip of paper. (For example, you might say, "Children with a 4-inch-high strip, find something taller than your strip of paper.")

Memory Coursing

*Children follow directions to move
around an established obstacle course.*

Skill Areas: directionality/prepositions; following directions; inferences; sentence usage; time concepts (*advanced level*); one-to-one correspondence; balance; body awareness; endurance; motor planning; auditory memory

Time Required: 30-40 minutes

Materials

equipment to create an obstacle course, such as:
    scooterboard
    blanket or pillow
    playground rope
    2 chairs
    hopping ball such as a Hoppity-Hop Ball®
    beanbags and target
simple pictures on index cards that depict how to move through each component of the obstacle course (each component can be used in more than one way)
5 index cards, each with a single number from 1-5 on it

Entry Level

Use any combination of materials to design an obstacle course that emphasizes prepositional concepts such as "under," "over," "around," "at," and "to." For example, tie the jump rope between two chairs for a child to belly crawl *under* the rope; place the blanket or pillow on the floor for a child to log roll *over;* have the children hop *around* the blanket or pillow on the hopping ball, throw beanbags *at* a target, or travel *to* the next obstacle on the scooterboard.

Have the first child select a numbered index card to determine how many picture cards the child will choose. (For example, "2" indicates that the child will pick up two picture cards.)

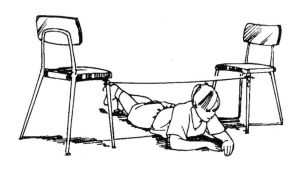

Without looking, the child selects the designated number of picture cards, then tells the class in complete sentences what actions are shown on the pictures. (For example, "I will hop *around* the pillow and crawl *under* the rope.")

The child proceeds to carry out the stated actions. The picture cards should remain within view so the child can refer to them if needed. The other children can also give verbal cues if the child forgets a step. The directions may be carried out in any order.

Intermediate Level

Conduct the activity in the same manner as the entry level, but remove the picture cards from view after the child has looked at them and stated the directions. Continue to allow the other children to offer verbal cues if the child needs them.

Advanced Level

Conduct the activity in the same manner as the entry level but, after the child has completed the obstacle course, ask questions about the order in which the child carried out the tasks. (For example, "What did you do after riding the scooterboard?") The other children can refresh the child's memory, if necessary.

Musical Ball

*Children practice color, letter, and number
recognition in conjunction with sequencing
as they play a ball game.*

Skill Areas: color, letter, and number recognition; patterns/sequencing; listening; body awareness; motor planning; visual memory; visual perception; auditory discrimination; matching

Time Required: 20-30 minutes

Materials

recorded music or a rhythm instrument
playground ball
2 sets of flash cards with sequences of 2-3 colored numbers or letters
2 sets of flash cards showing each number or letter in the sequences

Entry Level

The children stand or sit in a circle, a little more than one arm's length from their neighbors. Scatter one set of the flash cards showing individual numbers or letters face up in the middle of the circle. While you play music or a rhythm instrument, the children pass the ball around the circle. When you stop the music, the children stop passing the ball. Show the child who is left holding the ball a flash card with a letter or number on it. The child walks to the center of the circle and finds the matching card. That pair of flash cards is removed, and the game continues. Once the children understand the game, you can have them march around the circle while passing the ball.

Intermediate Level

The children pass the ball around the circle as long as the music plays. When you stop the music, show the child who is holding the ball a flash card with a sequence of two or three letters or numbers on it. Display the card for 2 to 4 seconds, then remove it from sight. The child walks to the center of the circle and finds the correct cards to duplicate the sequence. Have the class check the child's selections against the sequence card. If the sequence is incorrect, the class helps the child make the appropriate correction.

Advanced Level

When the music stops, show the child a flash card with a sequence of different colored letters or numbers on it. Display the card for 2 to 4 seconds, then remove it. The child walks to the center of the circle and selects the matching sequence card from memory. The class then checks to confirm that the two cards match in both the order and colors of the numbers (for example, a red 4 followed by a blue 6). If the sequence is incorrect, the class helps the child make the appropriate correction.

Variation: Once the children master this game, you can make it still more challenging. Place the cards showing individual letters or numbers face up in the center of the circle. Show the child a sequence card. Then have the child select the appropriate individual cards required to duplicate the sequence, both in terms of the items and their colors.

Musical Chair Descriptions

The children play a version of musical chairs while they practice giving descriptions.

Skill Areas: descriptor use; inferences; listening; sentence usage; body awareness; auditory discrimination

Time Required: 25-30 minutes

Materials

1 fewer chairs than there are students
rhythm instrument or recorded music
index cards, each with a child's name or photo on it (*entry activity*)
index cards, each picturing an object in the room (*intermediate and advanced levels*)
paper bag (to hold the index cards)

Entry Level

If you have access to an instant camera, take a picture of each child and mount it on an index card. If not, write each child's name on an index card. Place the index cards in the paper bag. Play "musical chairs" in the traditional way. The child who is left standing when the music stops picks a card from the bag. If necessary, whisper the name written on the card to the child so that the other children cannot hear you. The child gives a verbal description of the pictured or named child until one of the other children guesses who it is. The first child to guess correctly receives a gigantic "hip, hip, hooray."

Stress the rule that the children may not call one another names or use derogatory terms in their descriptions. Any child who is rude or hurtful to another child will not be allowed to continue playing.

Intermediate Level

Use pictures of classroom objects in place of pictures of children. The child who is left without a chair draws an object picture from the bag without allowing the other children to see it. The child gives three clues describing the color, the shape, and the feel (or quality) of the pictured object. (For example, if the pictured item is a red ball, the child might say, "It's red, it's round, and it's bouncy.") After *all three* clues have been given, the rest of the class guesses what the object is.

Advanced Level

The child who is left without a chair draws a picture of a classroom object from the paper bag. The child gives three clues that describe *how and when the object is used.* (For example, for a picture of a red ball, the child might say, "You take it to recess, you kick it, and you bounce it.") After *all three* clues have been given, the class guesses what the object is.

Name and Describe

*Children practice color and name recognition
as they speak in complete sentences and
become acquainted with classmates.*

Skill Areas: color recognition; name recognition; descriptor use; sentence usage; body awareness; motor planning

Time Required: 20-30 minutes

Materials
each child's name printed on a card

Entry Level
Sit in a circle with the entire class. Ask questions about the children's appearance and what they are wearing. For example, "Who is wearing brown shoes?" Call on one child to answer (or ask for a volunteer). Have the child answer in a complete sentence using the designated child's name. (For example, *"Wanda Lee* is wearing *brown* shoes.") Wanda Lee then stands up and shows the class her brown shoes.

Intermediate Level
Line up the cards with the children's names on them where everyone can see them (for example, along the chalk tray). One at a time, each child chooses a way to travel to his or her name card—by hopping, skipping, and so on. Upon reaching their names, the children hold up their name cards to show the class, report how they reached their names, and read their names aloud. (For example, "I hopped to my name. My name is Terry.")

Advanced Level
One at a time, the children move to and identify their names as in the intermediate level. Each child then introduces herself or himself (by first and last name) to a classmate. That classmate takes the next turn. For example, "Hi, Henry. My name is Bobby Chavez. You're next."

Name That Time

Children are introduced to time telling by creating a living clock and setting it to designated times.

Skill Areas: sentence usage; time concepts; number recognition; body awareness; visual perception; vocabulary

Time Required: 40 minutes

Materials

2 sets of 8½" x 11" cards, each with one number from 1-12 on it
2 lengths of string or cord, one about 12" shorter than the other
large clock with easily manipulable hands

Entry Level

Have 12 children volunteer to hold a number card. These children will serve as the numbers on the clock. As you call out each number in order from 1 to 12, the child with that number comes forward. Position these children in a circle so that each child's location corresponds to the location of that number on a real clock. Point out to the children which numbers are across the circle from each other—6 across from 12, 3 across from 9, 2 across from 8, and so on.

Describe general times of day—morning, noon, night, bedtime, for example—and talk about why people keep track of time.

Intermediate Level

Select one child to stand in the middle of the clock face holding one end of both lengths of cord. Have two other children each take the other end of one length of cord. Together these three children form the hands of the clock. Using the real clock, set the hands to a time that should be relatively familiar to the children (for example, 12:00 for lunchtime).

continued

The two children holding the outside ends of the "minute hand" and "hour hand" strings move to match the hands on the manipulable clock. (The third child remains in the center of the clock.) The class repeats after you the time and what occurs at that time. (For example, "It's 12:00 and that's lunchtime.")

Advanced Level

Use the manipulable clock to show the times at which regular events occur in the children's school day—for example, recess, lunch, dismissal. As you set the real clock to each of these times, do not tell the children what time you have set. Ask them to tell you the time and also what occurs at that time. Finally, have the children who make up the living clock duplicate the time that is on your clock.

Number Ball

Math Readiness

*While passing a playground ball,
children practice counting.*

Skill Areas: number recognition; one-to-one correspondence; oral counting; motor planning; visual motor; visual perception

Time Required: 20-30 minutes

Materials
playground ball
number flash cards

Entry Level
The children stand in two facing lines about three feet apart. The children pass the ball diagonally back and forth down the lines. With each pass of the ball, the children count up to a number you specify. You can have all the children count in unison or have only the child who receives the ball say that number, as long as each pass of the ball corresponds to a number.

Intermediate Level
Children pass the ball back and forth down the line as before. As each child receives the ball, show that child a number flash card. Have the child name the number before passing the ball on to the next child. If a flash card is incorrectly identified, still allow the child to pass the ball on. The next child to receive the ball attempts to name the same number. The children continue passing the ball and attempting to identify the same card until someone gives the correct answer. At that point, the ball is returned to the child who originally missed the number and is passed down the lines until all the children who missed that number have had an opportunity to name it correctly. Then continue the game showing a new flash card.

Advanced Level
In addition to naming the number, the child bounces and catches the ball that number of times while the entire class counts aloud.

Penny for Your Thoughts

*Children manipulate pennies
to learn the concepts "more" and "fewer"
while creating patterns with the pennies.*

Skill Areas: descriptor use; prediction; one-to-one correspondence; oral counting; motor planning; visual motor; visual perception (*advanced level*); comparatives/superlatives; linguistic concepts

Time Required: 30-45 minutes

Materials
handful of pennies for each child
circular objects 2½"-3" in diameter for tracing around
crayons, markers, or pencils
sheet of paper for each child

Entry Level
Give each child a blank piece of paper. Each child traces around a circular object such as a jar lid to make a circle in the middle of the sheet of paper. The children each take a handful of pennies and place them on the paper outside the circle. Using only the forefinger of the dominant hand, the children slide as many pennies as will fit within the boundaries of their circles.

Ask the children to visually compare the number of pennies inside and outside their circles. Have each child state whether there are more pennies inside or outside the circle. Next have the children practice counting to five by stacking the pennies inside and outside the circle in stacks of five.

Intermediate Level
Conduct the activity as in the entry level but have the children stack the pennies in sets of ten rather than five. Have the children turn their papers over to the blank side and arrange their pennies however they want (perhaps in a recognizable shape). Have them trace around each penny individually and then remove that penny from the paper. Once they have traced around all their pennies, ask the children to color as many of the circles as they wish to complete their pictures. You could have each child say whether more circles on the paper are colored or not colored.

Advanced Level

On the chalkboard, write down all the years in which the children were born (you will need to know this information). Have pairs of children who were born in the same year check their pennies for that date. If there are enough pennies, you may allow each child to keep one penny minted in the year of his or her birth. (The children can trade pennies if there are some pairs that have several pennies from the relevant years.)

Have the children stack 20 of the remaining pennies in two stacks of 5 and one stack of 10. Explain that if the children put the two stacks of 5 pennies together, that stack will be as high as the stack of 10 pennies. Have the children do this, then count the pennies in both stacks to confirm that each contains 10 pennies. This is merely an early introduction to addition and should not be the focus of the activity.

Pinning with a Song

The names and uses of body parts are addressed in a variation of "pin the tail on the donkey" and "hokey-pokey."

Skill Areas: body part identification; descriptor use; inferences; body awareness; motor planning; visual motor; auditory memory

Time Required: 30-45 minutes

Materials
    magazines with pictures of people
    glue
    scissors
    1-3 blindfolds (*intermediate level*)
    posterboard
    3 ribbons and straight pins

Entry Level
Review the names of body parts with the class, then divide the children into groups of two or three. Assign each child one or more body parts to find and give each group a supply of magazines and scissors. Have the class make a collage by cutting pictures of these body parts from magazines and gluing them on the posterboard. Secure the collage to a bulletin board or wall and have the children sit in a circle where they can see it.

One child pins a ribbon on any body part in the collage. The class names that body part, and the children rub that part on their own bodies. The children then stand up (still in the circle) and sing a chorus of "hokey-pokey" incorporating that body part. Continue as long as time allows.

Intermediate Level

Select a child to pin a ribbon to a body part on the collage. Blindfold the child first so that he or she cannot see which part has been pinned. Now ask a classmate to provide the blindfolded child with a clue about the part that is pinned. (For example, "You put a shoe on it.") With this clue, the blindfolded child tries to identify the pinned body part.

As this child returns to the circle, the rest of the class rubs the identified body part. Then the class performs the "hokey-pokey" using that body part.

Advanced Level

Conduct the activity as in the entry level except that two or three children sequentially pin ribbons to body parts on the collage. (The children are not blindfolded.) As they return to the circle, ask the other children to identify the functions of the "pinned" parts. (For an arm, they could say, "You wave it." For an elbow, they could say, "You bend it." For an eye, they could say, "You see with it.") The whole class then performs the "hokey-pokey" using the identified body parts in the sequence they were pinned.

Plates of Shapes

*Children trace, cut, and color shapes to reinforce
many academic concepts. These shapes are also used
in the "Plates of Shapes Revisited" activity.*

Skill Areas: color and shape recognition; same/different; descriptor use; following directions; one-to-one correspondence; balance; proximal stability; visual motor; comparatives/superlatives; linguistic concepts; matching

Time Required: 30-45 minutes

Materials
1 paper plate per pair of children (should be easy to cut)
scissors
2 large paper bags
several red, blue, and yellow crayons
1 set of large and 1 set of small circle, square, and triangle templates cut from heavy posterboard

Entry Level
Group the children into pairs. Give each pair a paper plate, crayons, scissors, and a choice of shape templates. Let the children choose their templates as long as the total number of large and small templates is roughly equal.

Have each pair of children work together to trace three shapes onto the paper plate, then color them and cut them out. Each child should do half of the tracing, cutting, and coloring. Encourage the children to work while half-lying on their stomachs and supporting themselves on their forearms.

Once all the children have traced, cut, and colored their shapes, ask each pair of children to examine their shapes and answer the following types of questions:
- Are any shapes exactly the same?
- Are any shapes the same size (that is, large or small)?
- Are any shapes the same color?

Intermediate Level

All the children sit in a circle. Place all the shapes in a paper bag and mix them up. Have each child select one shape. Pull a shape out of the paper bag yourself and ask the children questions that encourage them to compare their shapes to yours:

- Who has a circle that is larger than mine?

- Who has the same shape as mine?

- Who has a yellow triangle?

After asking each question, have the children with the shapes you asked for hop to you bringing their shapes. These children line up in front of the rest of the class holding up their shapes. Ask the class to verify whether all the shapes meet the criteria of your question. (For example, "Are all of these shapes smaller than mine?") **Note:** If a child's shape doesn't meet all the criteria, simply state how that shape differs from what you requested. (For example, "Shannon's circle is the same size as mine.") When the class has verified the shapes, the children in line may hop back to their places.

Advanced Level

Randomly divide the shapes into two separate paper bags and divide the class into two teams. The first two children in line hop to the bags (which should be 10 to 12 feet away from the lines). The two children select one shape each, then compare their shapes. Ask one child to describe how both shapes are the same and the other to describe how they are different. If you wish, ask other children in the class also to describe how the shapes are the same or different. The two children then hop back to their places with their shapes. Continue this process until all children have a shape.

continued

After everyone has selected a shape, have children arrange themselves in groups according to the shape, color, and/or size of their shapes. (For example, "Everyone with red shapes hop over here. Everyone with blue shapes hop over here. Everyone with yellow shapes hop over here.") Once the children have grouped themselves, ask them to compare the sizes of their groups. (For example, "Are there more red shapes than yellow shapes?" or "Are there fewer yellow shapes or blue shapes?")

Continue to have the children form groups based on different attributes of their shapes and then compare the sizes of their groups. If appropriate, you can have the children group themselves according to two or more criteria (for example, blue triangles or large red shapes).

Plates of Shapes Revisited

*Children use basic shapes to reinforce number
concepts and pre-reading skills (symbol inference).*

Skill Areas: color and shape recognition; prediction; sentence usage; number recognition; one-to-one correspondence; oral counting; balance; motor planning; visual motor; linguistic concepts

Time Required: 30-45 minutes

Materials
1 paper plate for each pair of children (should be easy to cut)
scissors
2 large paper bags
several red, blue, and yellow crayons
1 set of large and 1 set of small circle, square, and triangle templates cut
    from heavy posterboard
index cards

Entry Level
On each index card, write a number that the children can recognize. Have the children make two identical sets of shapes using the procedure described in "Plates of Shapes." (If they have already made one set of shapes for "Plates of Shapes," they need make only one more set.) Put all the cutout and colored shapes in a paper bag and place the bag 10 to 12 feet away from the children. Put the index cards with the single numbers written on them in the second paper bag.

continued

One at a time, each child draws a number out of the paper bag. Everyone names the number aloud. The child then chooses a corresponding number of children (that is, a 5 on the card means that the child selects five children). The selected children then all try to reach the paper bag holding the shapes in the number of jumps written on the number card (in this example, they would try to reach the paper bag in five jumps). You may wish to ask the children first whether they think they can make it to the bag in the designated number of jumps.

When the children reach the shape bag, each selects one shape, then they all line up so that the whole class can see their shapes. (The children can choose any shape they wish as long as each child takes only one shape.) Now ask the class questions that require counting the selected shapes. For example:

- "How many blue shapes are there?"

- "How many circles are there?"

- "How many big shapes are there?"

Intermediate Level

On the backs of the numbered index cards, draw a circle, triangle, or square *and* a stroke of one color (red, blue, or yellow). Have two or three children at a time log roll to the shape bag and select one shape each. Then they log roll back to their places holding the shapes straight over their heads.

After all children have selected one shape, place the remaining shapes in a pile on the floor. One child hops to the number bag and draws a card. The child names the number on the card, then turns it over and identifies the shape and color on the opposite side. The child asks for that number of children who have the designated shape in the correct color. (For example, "I need five children who have blue circles.") If more than the required number of children have the correct shape and color, the child may select which children will line up with their shapes. If there are fewer than the required number of children, these children line up. The "caller" then goes to the shape pile, selects however many shapes are needed to complete the set, and joins the line. Have the entire class verify that the resulting line-up does indeed match the color, shape, and number stipulations on the index card.

Advanced Level

Prepare index cards that have different numbers of shapes on one side (determine the number of shapes based on how high the children can count accurately). Depending on your children's abilities, you can make all the shapes on one index card identical or include a variety of shapes on the card. On the back of each index card, make a scribble of yellow, blue, or red.

Each child selects a shape as described in the intermediate level. The remaining shapes are then placed in a pile on the floor. One child selects an index card and counts the number of shapes on the card. The child asks the designated number of children who have the correct color of shape to stand up. (For example, if the card shows five circles on one side and the color blue on the reverse, the child would ask five children with blue circles to stand up). If too few or too many children stand up, the "caller" completes the set as described in the intermediate level.

Prep-O-Ball

Reading Readiness
Language and Listening

Children use playground balls to learn prepositions.

Skill Areas: directionality/prepositions; patterns/sequencing; descriptor use; body awareness; motor planning; auditory memory

Time Required: 20 minutes

Materials

2-3 playground balls

Entry Level

The children form two or three lines, with each child facing the back of the child in front. Give the first child in each line a ball. Call out a direction containing one of these prepositions: "under," "over," or "around." The children pass the ball over, under, or around their bodies to the child behind, according to your direction. Each child repeats the preposition while passing the ball. You can repeat one preposition for the entire line of children or you can give each child a different preposition. Possible directions include:

- over your head; over your shoulder

- under your leg; under your arm

- around your arm; around your waist; around your neck

Intermediate Level

Call out two of the prepositions "over," "under," and "around." The children must pass the ball all the way from the beginning to the end of the line using that pattern of movements. For example, if "over" and "around" are called, the first child passes the ball "over," the second passes it "around," and so on down the line.

Advanced Level

Call out a verbal sequence using all three of the prepositions "over," "under," and "around." The children pass the ball all the way down the line using this pattern of movements.

Variations: Once the children can remember the sequence of three passes without difficulty, you may also instruct them to pass the ball at different speeds (quickly, slowly, very fast, and so on) or to assume different positions while passing the ball (for example, kneeling or standing).

Prepositional Freeze

*Children practice using prepositions
during a game similar to "freeze tag."*

Skill Areas: directionality/prepositions; listening; sentence usage;
body awareness; motor planning; auditory discrimination

Time Required: 15-25 minutes

Materials

recorded music, rhythm instrument, or other noisemaker
masking tape or chairs to enclose an area of the classroom

Entry Level

Designate an area within which the children must remain while they run. As
long as you are playing music or making noise with the rhythm instrument,
the children run within the designated space. Children are not to touch one
another while they are running. As soon as the noise stops, the children must
freeze in place. Ask particular children forced-choice questions about their
locations with regard to other children. For example, you might ask, "Is Shana
or Carlos in front of you?"

Intermediate Level

Ask individual children open-ended questions about their locations with respect
to other children. For example, "Where is Rene?" The response would be,
"Next to me."

Advanced Level

Ask particular children to describe their locations with respect to two other
children. For example, "I am in front of Bobby and behind Susie."

Prepositions with Rhythm

*Children practice a variety of language
and listening skills while playing a game
similar to "musical chairs."*

Skill Areas: directionality/prepositions; same/different; following directions; sentence usage; body awareness; motor planning; auditory discrimination

Time Required: 15-20 minutes

Materials
chair for each child and the teacher
rhythm instrument

Entry Level
Arrange the chairs in a circle and have each child stand near a chair. Place your chair in the center of the circle. Model a variety of positions relative to your chair. (Stand in front of your chair, beside your chair, behind your chair, and so on.) Have the children follow your example and state where they are in relation to their chairs. (For example, "I am standing beside my chair.")

Begin playing the rhythm instrument and have the children walk around the circle of chairs until you stop playing. When you stop playing, call out and model a position (for example, "behind a chair"). The children stop walking, position themselves accordingly, then describe their position in unison in a complete sentence. (For example, "I am standing behind my chair.") Continue until you run out of time or the children have assumed all positions correctly.

Intermediate Level
Conduct as in the entry level. However, give the directions without modeling the correct position.

Advanced Level
When you stop beating the rhythm instrument, position yourself in relation to your chair and then say either "same" or "different." Depending on which word you say, the children will either duplicate your position or assume a different position. (Make sure that your orientation relative to the front, back, or side of the chair is clear to the children.)

Rhyme Time

*Children reinforce the concept
of rhyming through beanbag play.*

Skill Areas: rhyming; visual motor; auditory discrimination

Time Required: 15-20 minutes

Materials

2-3 beanbags or bean socks (see instructions for making bean socks on
page 30)

pairs of picture cards portraying rhyming words (ex: "moon" and "spoon")

Entry Level

Scatter the pictures face up in two groups on the floor, with the cards at least
two inches apart. Split the rhyming pairs so that one word is in one group and
its rhyme is in the other. Have the children line up in two teams, each team
approximately 10 feet away from one group of pictures.

The first child in each line throws a beanbag at that team's group of cards in
an attempt to hit one of the pictures. Pick up the pictures that the two children hit and name each one. The children repeat the words and state whether
or not they rhyme. Repeat the process until all the children have rotated
through their lines.

Intermediate Level

Place all of the pictures face down in one group, with one or two inches between the cards. Have the children sit in a circle surrounding the pictures.
Have two children aim the beanbags at the cards as in the entry level. However, when you pick up the cards, do *not* name the pictures. Instead, show
one picture and say two words, one that rhymes with the pictured word and
one that does not. Ask the children which of the words rhymes with the picture you are holding. Repeat for the second picture.

Advanced Level

Conduct the activity as in the intermediate level, but for each picture a child
hits, have the children provide at least two words that rhyme with it.

Scooterboard Flash

*While using scooterboards in a relay game,
children recall numbers and letters.*

Skill Areas: letter and number recognition; proximal stability; proprioception; visual and auditory memory; visual motor; visual perception

Time Required: 30-35 minutes

Materials
2 scooterboards
2 sets of number or letter flash cards
2 pads of paper and 2 pencils (*intermediate and advanced levels*)

Entry Level
The children divide into two teams and line up, each team with a scooterboard. Sit facing the children 10 to 12 feet away from where the two teams are lined up. Place four flash cards showing two different numbers and two different letters face up on the floor at either side of you (for a total of eight cards).

The first child in each line lies prone (on the stomach) on the scooterboard. Pick up one card from each side and show the cards to the children on the scooterboards for 3 or 4 seconds.

As soon as you put the cards back down, the children on the scooterboards propel themselves to the piles of cards using their arms only. (Children should try to keep their feet off the floor.) Each child selects the card you showed. When they have selected the correct cards, these two children propel themselves back to their lines, and the next child takes a turn.

Intermediate Level
Hold all the flash cards in your lap rather than scattering them on the floor. Place a pad of paper and a pencil on either side of you (and the same distance from both teams).

When the first two children have positioned themselves on their scooterboards, hold up one flash card so both children can see it for three or four seconds. *No one* is allowed to call out the number or letter on the flash card.

When you put the flash card down, each child races to that team's pad of paper. Both children write the number or letter you showed them (from memory) on the paper. (No peeking is allowed.)

After the children have written the number or letter, they check it with their teammates and with you. When everyone agrees that the number or letter is correct, and any corrections have been made in writing, the two children propel themselves back to their lines. Continue until everyone has had a turn.

Advanced Level

Conduct the activity as in the intermediate level but instead of showing a flash card, say the number or letter aloud.

Shopping Spree

Reading Readiness
Math Readiness

Children practice shape, color, number, and letter recognition as they improve visual memory and sequencing.

Skill Areas: color and shape recognition (*entry level*); letter and number recognition (*intermediate and advanced levels*); patterns and sequencing; balance; endurance; proprioception; visual memory; visual perception; reasoning

Time Required: 20-30 minutes

Materials
2-5 scooterboards (*optional*)
cards showing 1-3 shapes, colors, numbers, or letters
clock or stopwatch

Note: We recommend that you plant items around the room before this activity—for example, letterhead boards and books with letters or numbers on the cover.

Entry Level
The children break into two to five groups, then pair up within their groups. Each group decides which pair will go first. One member of the pair lies prone on the scooterboard with legs straight. The second child takes hold of the first child's ankles and will be pushing the child around. If you don't have access to scooterboards, you could tie the inside legs of each pair of children together and have them complete the activity as a three-legged race.

Show the first pair in each group a card with either a shape, a number, a letter, or a color on it. Each pair has 15 seconds to find and pick up an object with that item on it somewhere in the room. For example, if the card shows a circle, the children could find any round or circular object; if the card shows the color red, they may select any red item.

Each team who successfully finds an appropriate item within 15 seconds receives one point. Continue until all the pairs of children have had a turn. (Each pair should search for a different card.)

Intermediate Level

Conduct the activity in the same way, but show a flash card with two items on it (for example, the letter A and the number 2). The children have 20 seconds to find one object that contains an A then another object that contains a 2. They must select the objects in the order shown on the card.

Advanced Level

Conduct the activity in the same way, but show three items on each card. Allow the children to see the card for only 2 to 5 seconds. The children have 25 seconds to find three items with the features represented on the card. The children must remember the three items and their order while searching the classroom and must pick up the objects in the order they were represented on the card.

Strung Along

*Children use pieces of string to
physically act out the meanings of prepositions.*

Skill Areas: directionality/prepositions; inferences; sentence usage;
body awareness; motor planning

Time Required: 30 minutes

Materials

1 piece of string per child, approximately 30" long
pictures depicting the prepositions "under," "over," "next to," "around,"
and "on"

Entry Level

The children spread out so they are at least an arm's length apart. Hold up a
preposition picture and describe it to the children in a complete sentence. (For
example, "The rock is *on* the floor.") Each child duplicates this position relative to his or her body using the piece of string. For example, Alicia might
place her string *on* her shoe and Shana might place her string *on* her head.
Each child then describes the location of the string in a complete sentence.
("The string is *on* my shoe.")

Intermediate Level

Hold up a preposition picture and ask the children to duplicate it with their
pieces of string. Do not describe the picture first. The children state the locations of their pieces of string in complete sentences.

Advanced Level

The children work in pairs, with each child having a length of string. Hold up
a preposition picture and ask the children to duplicate the location relative to
their partner's body rather than their own. As a result, they must describe, in
a complete sentence, the location of their string relative to another person.
(For example, "My string is on Johnny's head.")

Stuff the Can

*Children work in pairs or groups
against a time limit to feel, count, and compare
fabric swatches they can or cannot see.*

Skill Areas: following directions; prediction; time concepts; one-to-one correspondence; oral counting; body awareness; proprioception; tactile; visual motor; problem solving

Time Required: 20-30 minutes

Materials
small cans with plastic lids; cut a ¼"-square opening in each lid
10-15 fabric swatches of varying thickness and textures
(approximately 1" square) for each group of children
blindfolds or handkerchiefs
number flash cards
10-second timer

Entry Level
Children work in pairs or small groups. Give each group one can and 10-15 fabric swatches. Ask each group of children to predict how many fabric swatches can be stuffed into the can within 10 seconds.

Once the groups have made their predictions, start the timer and have the children stuff as many swatches as they can through the opening in the lid using only the thumb and forefinger of their dominant hand. (You may need to cue the children to fold or roll up the swatches to fit them through the lid.) The children must not stick their fingers through the hole.

After 10 seconds, each group opens the can and counts how many fabric swatches are in it.

continued

Intermediate Level

Give each group a blindfold which is easy to remove (a handkerchief works well) and three or four number flash cards.

One child in the group shows another child a number flash card. The second child memorizes the number, then puts on the blindfold and attempts to stuff the can with that number of fabric pieces. Start the 10-second timer as soon as all the children have their blindfolds on. Continue until all the children have had a turn to stuff the can.

Advanced Level

Each group of children works together to stuff the can with fabric swatches that have specific qualities; for example, pieces of the same color, thick pieces, thin pieces, or pieces with many colors. Instruct the children to put a certain number of pieces of each type of fabric in the can. (For example, "Stuff your can with one thick and two thin pieces of cloth.")

Variation: As the children become proficient at this activity, have them select the fabrics while blindfolded.

Targeting Sounds

Children throw balls at targets representing sounds.

Skill Areas: letter recognition; phonics; visual motor; visual perception

Time Required: 15-30 minutes

Materials
2 playground balls (approximately 10" in diameter)
2 sets of letter flash cards
chalkboard and chalk

Entry Level
Have the children stand in two lines facing the chalkboard. Give the first child in each line a ball. Write two identical sets of three or four letters on the chalkboard, one set opposite each line. Stand where both lines of children can see you and hold up a letter flash card that corresponds to one of the letters on the board. All the children name the letter in unison.

continued

The first children in line throw their balls at the matching letter on the chalkboard. Regardless of whether the children hit the correct letter, they then go to the board and trace the correct letter with one finger. Meanwhile, the rest of the children trace the letter in the air and you model the sound of the letter.

Intermediate Level

Conduct the activity in the same manner as the entry level, but name one of the letters written on the chalkboard *without* showing a flash card of the letter.

Advanced Level

Say the sound represented by one of the letters on the chalkboard (without showing a flash card).

Telebounce Relay

Language and Listening

*Children practice listening skills by playing a game
of telephone that includes a motor component.*

Skill Areas: inferences; listening; sentence usage; balance; proximal stability;
motor planning; proprioception; auditory memory

Time Required: 20-40 minutes

Materials
2-4 hopping balls, such as Hoppity Hop Balls®
picture cards

Entry Level
Children line up in two to four teams, with plenty of space between teams.
Stand holding the picture cards at a spot equidistant from all teams of children. The first child from each line hops to you on the hopping ball. When
all the children have arrived, show them a picture card *without* allowing
the other children to see it. Describe something in the picture in a simple
sentence.

The children have to remember the sentence while riding back to the end of
their team's line. Each child whispers the sentence to the child at the end of
the line. Each child in turn whispers the sentence to the next child up the line
until the sentence reaches the front of the line. This child then hops to you
on the ball and whispers the sentence to you. After all the teams have reported
their sentences back to you, show the picture card to the class and repeat all
the sentences told to you. The entire class decides how accurately the messages were transmitted.

Show the messengers a different picture card and give them a new sentence.
Continue until each child has had a turn.

continued

Intermediate Level

Conduct the activity in the same way as the entry level, but let the messengers make up their own sentences about the picture card. You might wish to have each child dictate the sentence to you before returning to the team, so you have a record of their original messages. Each team relays the message up the line and back to you as described for the entry level. Read each team's original sentence and the sentence relayed back to you. The entire class decides whether the sentence was relayed correctly. If not, the class then decides whether the transformed sentence still reflects something in the picture card.

Advanced Level

One child from each team hops to you on a ball and makes up a sentence about a picture card as described in the intermediate level. However, on returning to the team, the messenger relays the message to the child at the *front* of the line. The messenger then goes to the end of the line and waits for the message to reach him or her. When the sentence reaches the end of the line, the messenger repeats it and then reports whether or not the sentence has changed.

This Is the Way We . . .

*Children use a familiar melody to practice
a variety of motor acts and language skills.*

Skill Areas: following directions; inferences (*advanced level*);
sentence usage; body awareness; motor planning; body language

Time Required: 30 minutes

Materials
action pictures of people doing familiar tasks
paper bag (*advanced level*)

Entry Level
Rehearse the traditional children's song "This Is the Way We Wash Our Clothes" to ensure that all the children are familiar with the melody and the basic format of the verses. Now substitute a variety of different actions for the ones in the original song. Have the class sing in unison while pantomiming the action. Here are some suggestions:

stomp our feet	chop some wood
brush our teeth	eat spaghetti
wash our faces	look at books
pat our elbows	eat ice cream
climb a ladder	jump rope
swing on swings	ride a horse

The more advanced the children are, the more abstract the actions you can give them.

Intermediate Level
Whisper in one child's ear the key phrase of the verse. The child pantomimes the action in front of the class (without singing). The rest of the class tries to guess what the action is before they join in and sing the song using the actions pantomimed by the child.

Advanced Level
The child draws an action picture from the bag and attempts to act it out before making up a phrase about the picture. Once the class guesses what the action is, they all sing in unison while pantomiming it.

Walking the Plank

*Children walk along a balance beam
and perform visual-perceptual tasks such as
figure-ground discrimination, identifying hidden
pictures, or identifying visual absurdities.*

Skill Areas: directionality/prepositions; sentence usage; balance; motor
planning; visual perception; problem solving

Time Required: 20-30 minutes

Materials

balance beam (or a piece of masking tape stretched along the floor)
variety of pictures that have hidden objects (such as those found in the
magazine *Highlights*), books similar to the *Where's Waldo?* books, or
simple worksheets that involve finding matching pictures
blindfold (*advanced level*)

Entry Level

One at a time, children walk down the balance beam or the tape line. When
they reach the end, you show them a picture in which they must find or identify
a certain object. Use a simple picture in which the children can find the matching or hidden object fairly easily. You may need to give general cues such as,
"Look near the top of the picture," as well as imposing a reasonable time limit.

Intermediate Level

Vary the manner in which the children travel down the beam to reach the
picture (for example, walking backwards). After the child finds the target
object in the picture, model a sentence describing its location. For example,
"That's right. Waldo is in the upper left-hand corner." (Even if the children do
not know the concepts of right and left, this will begin exposing them to these
directions.)

Advanced Level

Have each child walk the beam wearing a blindfold. On reaching the end, the
child removes the blindfold to look at the picture. On finding the hidden object, the child describes its location to you as completely as possible. For example, "Waldo is in the top half of the (right) page."

Wheelbarrow Memory

*Children practice memory and sequencing skills
while having a wheelbarrow race.*

Skill Areas: patterns/sequencing; body awareness; proximal stability; motor
planning; proprioception; visual and auditory memory; linguistic concepts

Time Required: 20-40 minutes

Materials
2 identical sets of cards, each showing 2-4 objects

Entry Level
Use the set of two-item sequence cards. Cut up one set of cards so that every
object is separate. For example, a card showing an apple and a banana would
be cut into two cards, one with an apple and the other with a banana. Leave
the matching set of cards intact.

Divide the class into two or three groups. Place all of the cut-apart pictures
face up in a pile on the floor. Have the children within each team pair up so
that they can form human wheelbarrows. (The first child walks on two hands
while the second child supports the first child's feet.)

Show the first pair on each team an (intact) card showing a sequence of
objects. Have all the children name the objects in order from left to right.
Stress concepts such as "first" and "last" for describing the order of the objects. The pairs then form wheelbarrows and move to the pile of individual
pictures. They find the objects that were on the sequence card and reassemble
the card.

Intermediate Level
Conduct the activity in the same way using three-item sequence cards. Introduce the term "middle" for describing the order of items in the sequences.

Advanced Level
Use four-item sequence cards. You may want to introduce the concepts "first,"
"next," and "last."

Wheelbarrow Numbers

*Children practice identifying, counting, and writing
numbers within the context of a wheelbarrow race.*

Skill Areas: number recognition; one-to-one correspondence; oral counting;
body awareness; proximal stability; motor planning; proprioception; visual
motor; matching

Time Required: 30-40 minutes

Materials
2 sets of number flash cards
box or other container
approximately 20 identical manipulatives such as 1" cubes,
    clothespins, or straws
chalkboard and chalk

Entry Level
Group the manipulatives in sets of one to five objects. Place a number flash
card in front of each set identifying how many items are in it. Have the children line up in pairs about 10 feet away from the sets of objects.

The first pair of children forms a human wheelbarrow. Show the pair a number flash card. The two children move to that set of manipulatives and pick
up the index card from in front of it. Remaining as a wheelbarrow, they move
to the chalkboard. One child copies the number on the board while the other
child makes that number of slashes on the board. The child who is making
the slashes should attempt to draw the correct number without having to point
to and count each one. These two children return to the end of the line while
you replace the flash card in front of the set of objects.

Intermediate Level

Say a number aloud to the pair of children (without showing them a flash card). Have them complete the activity as in the entry level.

Advanced Level

Remove the index cards from in front of the sets of manipulatives.

Note: You may wish to provide quiet work that the children can be doing while waiting for their turns. For example, the children might

- draw numbers in the air

- form numbers out of clay

- count using manipulatives

Word Hopping

*Children practice hopping
while they identify letters and sounds.*

Skill Areas: letter recognition; phonics; rhyming; sentence usage; balance; endurance; motor planning

Time Required: 30 minutes

Materials
hopping ball, such as a Hoppity Hop Ball®
2 sets of letter flash cards
chalkboard and chalk (*advanced level*)

Entry Level
Have the children line up single file. Place two or three letter flash cards on the floor 10 to 15 feet away from the line of children. Hold up a letter flash card. The first child in line hops to the flash cards on the floor, finds the matching letter, and names it. Ask the child whether that letter is in his or her first or last name. The child hops back to the line carrying the letter flash card. All the other children in line determine whether that letter occurs in their names. In unison, the children recite the alphabet as far as that letter.

Intermediate Level
Instead of showing a flash card, say a letter sound. The child hops up and chooses the corresponding letter card. When the child has selected the correct letter, say two words, one of which begins with the child's letter. The child has to identify which word begins with the target sound. The child hops back to the line and repeats the sound and the word that begins with that sound. Depending on the level of your class, you may have each child in line contribute one of the following:

- a word that rhymes with the child's word
- another word that begins with the same letter
- a sentence containing the child's word

Advanced Level
Say a sound. The first child in line hops to the chalkboard on the ball, writes the corresponding letter, and thinks of a word beginning with that letter.

JIFFIES

EXCITATORY ACTIVITIES

CALMING ACTIVITIES

Jiffies

Use these Jiffies when you have a few minutes of "empty" time and don't want to lose the children's attention or waste the time. These activities are ideal for all the times when children have to wait in line—going to recess, the cafeteria, the library, waiting for dismissal, and so on.

Appliance Alive

Skill Areas: descriptor use; body awareness; motor planning; body language

Time Required: 4-5 minutes

Materials: pictures of various appliances (optional)

Directions

1. Mention an appliance with which the children are familiar. (If some children are unfamiliar with that appliance, show a picture of it and explain how it works.)

2. Ask the children to pretend they are that appliance, imitating the noise the appliance would make and, if applicable, imitating its moving parts.

3. If time allows, expand the activity by introducing more detailed pantomimes. When pretending to be a washing machine, for example, the children can collect "clothes" (any objects) of the same color. They can pretend to be clothes being washed in hot and cold water on fast and slow cycles. They can imitate the spin cycle, and so on.

Echo Clap

Skill Areas: patterns/sequencing; listening; body awareness; motor planning; tactile; auditory discrimination

Time Required: 3-5 minutes

Materials: none

Directions

1. Stand facing the children. Demonstrate how to clap your hands, slap your thighs, and snap your fingers. Make sure that the children can name these three actions.

2. Turn your back and either clap, slap, or snap (or any combination of the three, depending on your children's listening skills).

3. Ask the children to identify which noise or noises you made (without having seen you make the noise).

4. If they are able, have them duplicate the noise or sequence of noises.

Flamingo Fandango

> Reading Readiness
> Math Readiness

Skill Areas: directionality/prepositions; one-to-one correspondence; oral counting; balance; body awareness; motor planning; body language

Time Required: 3-5 minutes

Materials: a picture of a flamingo standing on one leg (optional)

Directions

1. Show the children the picture of the flamingo, or describe to them what one looks like.

2. Have them pretend to be flamingos. They make their arms into wings by placing their right hands under their right armpits and their left hands under their left armpits. Next have them place their left feet against their right knees so they are standing on one foot.

3. Call out a number and ask the children to "flap their wings" or "peck for food" that number of times. After a few minutes, have the children switch to their left legs.

4. You can begin introducing the concepts of right and left by asking the children to do actions with only their right or left arms or legs.

Hop to It

Skill Areas: color, letter, or number recognition; descriptor use; sentence usage; balance; motor planning; matching

Time Required: 4-5 minutes

Materials: flash cards or pictures of objects, colors, numbers, or letters that are present in the room

Directions
1. Show a picture or flash card to a child. Ask the child to hop to the object and tell you either what it is, what color it is, or its purpose. Then the child hops back.

2. You can have children use different modes of traveling to the objects— walking on tiptoe, jumping, walking backwards, and so on.

I Am Going . . .

Skill Areas: object classification; sentence usage; auditory memory

Time Required: 4-5 minutes

Materials: none

Directions

1. Give the children a destination. Ask them what they will need to take with them when they go or what they will see or do when they get there. Each child must repeat everything the preceding children have said and add an item to the list.

2. Children must speak in complete sentences. For example, given the destination "the zoo," the first child might respond, "I am going to the zoo, and I will see a monkey." The next child might say, "I am going to the zoo, and I will see a monkey and a giraffe." As the list gets longer, all children may help recall the items.

3. When the list becomes too long for the children to remember, begin a new category. You can make this activity easier or more challenging, depending on the topic you introduce.

Rhyming Hops

Skill Areas: rhyming; balance; motor planning

Time Required: 3-5 minutes

Materials: none

Directions

1. Say two rhyming words.
2. The children repeat the two words, jumping as they say each one.
3. Vary the speed with which the children jump and say the words.
4. Vary whether the children jump in place, jump forward, jump backwards, and so on.
5. For children who are able to rhyme, have them select the pairs of words to which they jump.

Same Noise/Different Noise

Skill Areas: same/different; listening; auditory discrimination

Time Required: 3-5 minutes

Materials: a variety of small objects which make different sounds, such as cellophane, a rattle, and keys

Directions

1. Allow the children to watch you make noise with each item.
2. Turn your back so the children cannot see you using the noisemakers. Make two sounds using either two different objects or the same object twice.
3. Ask the children whether the noises were the same or different.

Shrinking Animals

Skill Areas: descriptor use; auditory discrimination; auditory memory; reasoning

Time Required: 3-5 minutes

Materials: none

Directions

1. Name an animal with which the children are fairly familiar, such as a dog.

2. Ask the children to make the noise a very large example of that animal would make. ("Bark like a large dog.") You may want to specify how many times the children should make the noise. ("Bark three times like a large dog.")

3. Next ask them to make the sound a medium-sized example of that animal would make. ("Bark like a medium-sized dog.")

4. Finally, ask them to make the sound a small-sized example of that animal would make. ("Bark like a small dog.")

5. Discuss with the children how these three sounds are different. If space permits, you may wish to have them assume the postures of large, medium, and small animals.

Siren Singing

Language and Listening

Skill Areas: descriptor use; body awareness; motor planning; body language

Time Required: 2-3 minutes

Materials: none

Directions

Have the children imitate a siren noise (perhaps pretending to be police cars). Instruct them to glide their voices from low to high and back to low pitches on your command. As the children's voices glide upward, have them stretch their arms and bodies as high as they can. As they glide down to a low pitch, have them slowly crouch. Bear in mind that high pitches will tend to be excitatory.

Vocal Play

Reading Readiness

Skill Areas: phonics; oral motor

Time Required: 2-3 minutes

Materials: letter flash cards

Directions

1. Use the familiar melody children use when teasing each other. Change the first consonant of each syllable to the sound of the letter you are holding up. For example, L would be chanted as "La-la la-la la la."

2. Have the children vary the pitch, speed, and volume of their chanting. Bear in mind that loud or fast chanting will tend to raise children's energy levels whereas quiet, slow chanting will be more calming.

la-la la - la la la

Excitatory Activities

The excitatory activities are useful for a transition from a quiet, focused activity to a more active one or when you want to give the children a "move-around-and-stretch break." Another time to try these activities is when childrens' energy levels are low—for example, after a snack or meal or late in the day. Most also enhance body awareness. Although these activities are intended to raise children's activity levels, do not let them get out of control. Any fast and arrhythmical activities are typically excitatory; we encourage you to try developing your own or consult your school occupational or physical therapist for additional ideas.

The Boxer

Time Required: 2-4 minutes

Materials: none

Directions
1. Have children stand where they have plenty of free space around them.
2. Show them how to "air box" much like professional boxers do. Vary the speed with which they "throw punches" and call out the direction in which they are to punch—for example, "up-up," "side-side," "down-down."
3. Once the children have mastered the arm movements, you can add different kinds of boxing footwork.

Hurry and Go Nowhere

Time Required: 2-4 minutes

Materials: none

Directions
1. Children run in place while vocalizing with some continuous noise. One noise the children like is to blow through their lips—rather like blowing a raspberry.
2. Vary the speed and volume of the vocalizations. The faster and louder the noise, the more excitatory the activity.

Jump to It

Time Required: 2-3 minutes

Materials: none

Directions
1. Children stand at least an arm's length apart. They jump up and down in place while chanting "jump" in time with each jump.
2. Change the action to hopping and have them chant "hop." Then have the children switch feet and continue hopping.
3. If the children become adept at jumping and hopping in place, have them form a circle and jump or hop while moving around the circle.

Logging Time

Time Required: 4-5 minutes

Materials: small objects the children can hold

Directions
1. Have the children lie on the floor with enough room between them to stretch out with their arms over their heads. Give each child a small object to hold overhead while rolling. The children stretch out full length and log roll while holding the objects over their heads.
2. While they are rolling, the children chant, "log-alog-alog."

Slap Happy

Time Required: 3-5 minutes

Materials: none

Directions
1. Demonstrate the following sequence of motions: clap, slap your thighs, and cross your arms in front of your body to pat the opposite shoulder.
2. Have the children stand and imitate this sequence. Increase the intensity and speed of these actions as the children learn the sequence.
3. You may want to give the children a number of times to perform each action in the sequence. If, for example, you say "5," they will do five claps, five slaps, and five pats. Have them count aloud as they do the actions.

Cheers

To contribute to children's development of self-esteem (a vital component of healthy development) we have provided two cheers. You can use these cheers for positive reinforcement during any of the *Multi-Play* activities, or indeed, at any time throughout your daily schedule.

We have provided only two suggestions because part of this activity is to have children develop their own repertoire of cheers. We focus on having children invent a sequence of controlled motor movements; whether to have them add a verbal component to the cheer is at your discretion.

Hip, Hip, Hooray

1. Children stand with their arms spread out to their sides at a 90-degree angle. (Incidentally, notice how many children can maintain this arm position without complaining and without letting their arms slowly drop to their sides.)

2. The children slowly bend their right arm to touch their hand to their right shoulder while saying "hip."

3. Keeping their right hand on the right shoulder, they do the same motion with the left arm during the second "hip."

4. They raise both arms straight up in the air and jump as high as they can while yelling "hooray!"

5. Try having them repeat the cheer three times in a row, and try to incorporate different children's names in the cheer.

Yea, Friend

1. The children squat with both arms bent in front of them. They circle one forearm around the other (the movement used in the rhyme "This Old Man Came Rolling Home"). At the same time, the children give a long "yea," gradually increasing the volume and pitch as they slowly rise from a squat to a standing position.

2. When they reach standing position, the children jump up and yell the name of the child they are applauding. (For example, "Y-E-A PAM!")

3. The children can make up a different cheer for each day of the week, or you can have cheerleaders who lead the cheers on different days of the week (much like line leaders).

Calming Activities

Try one of these activities when children are especially active and disorganized and have to make the transition to an activity requiring focused attention and limited motor activity. Any type of repetitive, rhythmical, slow task is generally calming, as is any activity where the children pretend to be moving or carrying something heavy. We encourage you to try inventing your own calming activities to supplement these. Your school occupational or physical therapist can help you if you have questions.

A Bigger Room

Time Required: 2-5 minutes

Materials: walls that are bare at the children's shoulder height

Directions
1. Each child finds an open space along a wall. They stand facing the wall with arms straight out in front of them at shoulder height. Have the children all push together against the wall, as if trying to make the room bigger.
2. If time permits, children may remove their shoes and do the same with their feet.

Burrito Wrap

Time Required: 3-5 minutes

Materials: large towel or soft blanket for each child

Directions
1. Children wrap themselves in their blankets as tightly as they can and lie or sit quietly.
2. If you have enough assistants, place each child on an open blanket. Wrap up all the children with their arms bent close to their faces.
3. For a particularly active child, have the child perform a task requiring attention *while* wrapped up.

Circle Push

Time Required: 2-5 minutes

Materials: none

Directions
1. Children form a circle facing inward. They extend both arms out to their sides, so that their palms touch those of the children on either side.
2. Each child pushes against the palms of the neighboring children. If the children are sufficiently coordinated, they can sway back and forth while pushing against one another.
3. If time permits, have pairs of children sit down facing each other. (They can remain in a circle.)
4. The children lean back on their elbows with legs straight and the soles of their feet touching. Each child pushes against the other's feet, much as they did with their hands.

Hanging Out

Time Required: 3-5 minutes

Materials: monkey bars or similar equipment from which children can hang by their hands

Directions
Have each child grab a bar and dangle limply from it. Do not allow them to actively swing back and forth.

Low Drone

Time Required: 1-2 minutes

Materials: none

Directions
Have the children hum in a low, continuous drone. Stress that they should keep the sound quiet and low-pitched.

Moving Company

Time Required: 3-5 minutes

Materials: heavy furniture

Directions

Children push or pull furniture around the room. Make certain that the furniture is not so heavy as to injure children. It should be heavy enough to provide only moderate resistance.

One-Person Tug-o-War

Time Required: 2-5 minutes

Materials: 1 long piece of rope so that each child can grab roughly 18 inches of it, or individual lengths of rope for each child

Directions

1. Every child grabs one end of the rope in each hand (hands approximately 12 inches apart).

2. The children pull in opposite directions with each hand, as if having a tug-o-war with themselves.

Materials List

This list gives all the materials used for all the activities in *Multi-Play*. Most of the materials on this list are readily available in the classroom, can be provided by students, or can be accumulated gradually over the year.

- Alphabet line
- Balance beam (optional)
- Balloons (different sizes, shapes, and colors)
- Balls (playground, tennis, and sponge balls)
- Beanbags (and optional target)
- Beans, lentils, popcorn, and other beanbag fillings
- Blankets or large towels (one for each child)
- Blindfolds or handkerchiefs (enough for ½ your students)
- Boxes, containers, or paper bags to hold cards
- Cans (small) with plastic lids (enough for ½ to ¼ of the class)
- Chairs
- Chalkboard and chalk
- Circular objects to trace around
- Clock with manipulable hands
- Clothespins (optional)
- Coffee cans (1 pound) with plastic lids (1 per child)
- Corrugated cardboard (to make shapes if you don't have wooden shapes)
- Cotton balls dyed various colors
- Dowels (or other lightweight, sturdy sticks or tubes)
- Fabric scraps in a variety of textures
- Flash cards (2 sets of each) with numbers, letters, and colors
- Flash cards with the children's names
- Glue

- Hoppity-Hop Balls® or other brand of hopping ball (at least 2); these can be purchased fairly inexpensively at large toy stores.
- Index cards
- Jars and cans in a variety of sizes with matching lids
- Macrame cord ($^1/_2$" or less in diameter)
- Magazines for cutting pictures from
- Magnets (2-4 small sized)
- Masking tape
- Measuring cups
- Objects: small manipulables (20 identical objects about 1" in size); also pairs of objects
- Paper: $8^1/_2$" x 11" writing tablets and construction paper
- Paper bags (some large enough to fit over children's heads)
- Paper clips of varying sizes
- Paper plates
- Pencils, crayons, markers, and chalk
- Pennies. You could ask each child to bring in 50¢ worth of pennies, or get roughly $10 worth of rolled coins from the bank. If children bring in their own pennies, return them at the end of the school year.
- Pictures

  of actions
  of various wild and domesticated animals
  of appliances
  of common objects, particularly those found in a classroom
      (2 identical sets)
  of a house, farm or barn, and zoo
  of different locations in the community
  of different occupations
  of pairs of rhyming words
  illustrating prepositions
  containing hidden objects
- Plastic and metal eating utensils
- Posterboard or tagboard
- Rhythm instruments and noisemakers

- Ribbons
- Rope, at least 15 feet long
- Rubber bands
- Rulers
- Safety pins
- Scale
- Scissors (child-size and adult)
- Scooterboards (as many as possible). These can be ordered or made; ask your school therapist for ordering information. Instructions for making a scooterboard are given in the appendix.
- Socks (1 per child)
- Straight pins
- Straws
- String (at least 1 roll of heavy duty)
- Timer or stopwatch
- Wooden circles, squares, and triangles (enough for each child to have a set)

Appendix:
Directions for Making
a Scooterboard

You can make scooterboards in a variety of sizes to fit the heights and weights of your students. You probably will not want to make the scooterboard smaller than 11" x 13" unless you are working with children who are very small. Bear in mind that the larger the scooterboard, the less effort a child has to expend to keep his or her body off the floor.

Note: Always stress that the children should *never* stand on a scooterboard.

Materials Required
   wood at least 11" x 13" x 1"
   foam scrap roughly ¹/₂" thick
   carpet scraps
   4 caster wheels 4" in diameter (the type with a plastic ring around the
      wheel)
   16 wood screws
   wood glue
   clamps (optional)

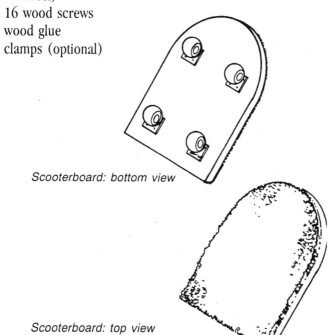

Scooterboard: bottom view

Scooterboard: top view

continued

Directions

1. Shape the piece of wood so it is narrower and rounded toward the front (see diagram).

2. Cut the foam to the same size as the wood.

3. Cut a scrap of carpet that is two inches larger than the wood all around.

4. Use wood screws to attach the casters to the underside of the wood in roughly the locations shown in the diagram.

5. Spread a generous amount of glue along all borders of the underside of the scooterboard where you will attach the carpet.

6. Center the foam and then the carpet on the top side of the scooterboard. Pull the carpet as tight as you can and turn it under the scooterboard on all sides. Use clamps to hold the carpet in place until the glue dries.

Glossary

The terms defined in this glossary appear in the skill areas and activity descriptions. Although these are technical terms used in occupational therapy and speech-language pathology, we have chosen to define them here because the concepts all relate to a child's ability to pay attention, use writing instruments, and learn basic concepts. The definitions here are fairly general and nontechnical, so we encourage you to contact your school therapists for further information.

Auditory Discrimination: Ability to differentiate and compare sounds.

Auditory Memory: Capacity to remember what was heard.

Balance/Equilibrium: Ability to use movements to regain midline.

Body Awareness: Perception of one's body and where it is located in space; vision is not necessary for a good and functional body awareness.

Fine Motor: Use of small muscle groups, particularly in the hands and fingers, for skilled, precise activities.

Linguistic Concepts: Words used to define or describe ideas, such as spatial terms ("between," "in front," "across") and temporal words ("hour," "tomorrow," "afternoon").

Motor Planning: The ability to develop an idea for an intended movement, to organize this idea into a motor action, and to carry out the action.

Phonics: Method of teaching reading by teaching the sounds associated with particular letters or letter combinations.

Problem Solving: Any of several thinking skills that include drawing inferences, anticipating and avoiding problems, determining the cause of events, and reasoning a solution to a problem.

Proprioception: The sensations received by muscles and joints that let one know how and when joints are changing position or when muscles are contracting o stretching.

Proximal Stability: Steadiness within the trunk, pelvic girdle, and shoulder girdle that allows one to effectively use one's arms, hands, and legs away from the body. Proximal stability is necessary for maintaining an upright posture while sitting or standing.

Temporal Concepts: Ideas relating to the passage of time, including general terms such as "morning," "week," "first," "last," and "yesterday," as well as telling specific times.

Visual Closure: The ability to imagine how an incomplete visual image would be completed.

Visual Discrimination: Ability to differentiate and compare things that are seen.

Visual Motor: The act of using sight to guide the body through the execution of a motor activity.

Visual Perception: The meaning or interpretation that the brain gives to visual input. (A person can have good vision without having good visual perception.)

Visual Tracking: The movement of the eyes as they follow a moving object.

Vocabulary

> **Expressive:** Ability to use words and concepts to communicate. Expressive vocabulary skills include naming items and using terms to describe or define things.

> **Receptive:** Understanding of words and concepts. Receptive vocabulary skills include recognizing named pictures and understanding directions.

Word Associations: Connections between seemingly unrelated words that are made on the basis of world knowledge. For example, "rain," "Easter," "birds," and "daffodils" are all associated with springtime.

Suggested Reading

Ayres, A. J. 1972. Improving academic scores through sensory integration. *Journal of Learning Disabilities* 5:336-43.

_____. 1973. *Sensory integration and learning disorders.* Los Angeles: Western Psychological Services.

_____. 1979. *Sensory integration and the child.* Los Angeles: Western Psychological Services.

_____. 1985. *Developmental dyspraxia and adult onset apraxia.* Torrance, CA: Sensory Integration International.

Beadle, M. 1971. *A child's mind: Children learn during the critical years from birth to age five.* New York: Doubleday.

de Quiros, J. B., and O. L. Schrager. 1979. *Neuropsychological fundamentals in learning disabilities.* San Diego, CA: Academic Therapy Publications.

Fernald, G. 1943. *Remedial techniques in basic school subjects.* New York: McGraw-Hill.

Fisher, A. C., E. A. Murray, and A. C. Bundy. 1991. *Sensory integration theory and practice.* Philadelphia, PA: F. A. Davis Co.

Frostig, M., and D. Horne. 1964. *The Frostig program for the development of visual perception: Teacher's guide.* New York: Follett, a division of Simon and Schuster.

Gessell, A. 1940. *The first five years of life: The pre-school years.* New York: Harper and Row.

Hanson, R. A., and R. Reynolds. 1980. *Child development.* St. Paul, MN: West Publishing Co.

Llinas, R. R. 1990. *The workings of the brain: Development, memory, and perception.* New York: W. H. Freeman and Co.

Nolte, J. 1989. *Study guide to accompany the human brain.* St. Louis, MO: C. V. Mosby Company.

Pines, M. 1967. *Revolution in learning: The years from birth to six.* New York: Harper and Row.

Pope, L. 1982. *Guidelines for teaching students with learning problems.* North Bergen, NJ: Book-Lab.

Schwartz, M. S. 1985. *Therapy as learning.* Dubuque, IA: Kendall/Hunt Publishing Co.

Add these movement products to your sensory-motor therapy program . . .

SENSORY-MOTOR INTEGRATION ACTIVITIES
by Barbara E. Fink, OTR

Help your clients improve their sensory-motor integration and development with these creative activities. You'll have reproducible therapy plans emphasizing abilities such as touch, equilibrium, and bilateral motor coordination. Each plan can be individualized and includes a discussion of objectives, procedure, and measurement.

Catalog No. 4160-Y   **$39**

SENSEABILITIES
Understanding Sensory Integration
by Maryann Colby Trott, M.A., with Marci Laurel,
M.A., CCC-SLP, and Susan L. Windeck, M.S., OTR/L

Educate parents and teachers about sensory integration with this easy-to-understand training resource. Give them practical information they can apply to real-life situations. Activities encourage children to move across all sensory domains without realizing it! Reproduce all or part of the material including chapters on the tactile and vestibular system, therapy session, school, and more.

Catalog No. 4283-Y   **$59**

EXTRAORDINARY PLAY WITH ORDINARY THINGS
Recycling Everyday Materials to Build Motor Skills
by Barbara Sher, M.A., OTR

Learn how you can recycle materials in a broad variety of games and therapeutic activities. Use for home visits, in the clinic and regular classroom, and with mainstreamed special needs children 4-12 years old. Each chapter lists ideas for games to play using different types of reusable items. Chapters include—Newspapers, Milk and Other Cartons, Cans, Paper, Lids, Wood, and more!

Catalog No. 4738-Y   **$39**

Therapy Skill Builders
A division of
Communication Skill Builders
3830 E. Bellevue/P.O. Box 42050
Tucson, Arizona 85733/(602) 323-7500